904/07

D0383970

YOU CAN
COMPETE

Santa Maria Public Library
Presented by

Scheryn Pratt

6/07

YOU CAN COMPETE

DOUBLE SALES WITHOUT DISCOUNTING

BOB PHIBBS

BRIXTON MANOR PUBLISHING

Published by Brixton Manor Publishing
3040 E. First St.
Long Beach, CA 90803
www.retaildoc.com

Publisher's Cataloging-in-Publication Data
Phibbs, Bob
    You can compete : doublesales without discounting / by Bob Phibbs.
    –2nd ed. –Long beach, CA : Brixton Manor, 2003

    p ; cm.

    ISBN 0-9709984-1-4

    1. Sales management. 2. Selling. 3. Retail trade.

HF5438.4 .P55 2003   2002115602
658.81—dc21   0301

www.bookpublishing.com
Cover design by Kathie Collins
Interior design by Barbara Hodge

This publication is designed to provide accurate and authoritative information in regard to the subject matter covered. It is sold with the understanding that the publisher is not engaged in rendering legal or accounting services. If legal advice or other expert assistance is required, the services of a competent professional should be sought.

Printed in the United States of America

07 06 05 04 03 * 6 5 4 3 2

Dedication

To
Bill Pratt and Fred Pratt, my first clients,
and to my parents

Contents

Foreword

When I wrote this book two years ago, the marketplace was optimistic. The stock market was still at stratospheric heights, unemployment was low and America faced no serious challenges. Then the stock market melted down, beginning with the bust of the dot.com industries, whose much-hyped destruction of brick and mortar stores never materialized. At the same time a divisive and muddied presidential election splintered the country's confidence. Things had started to look troubling. And then came September 11.

The most immediate casualty was consumer confidence. Everyone dealing in the retail, restaurant or travel industry suffered because people simply stopped shopping. Faced with the news that shoppers were pulling back, retailers prepared for a dismal holiday season.

While dire predictions of losses of 20 percent were plentiful, sales still posted gains over the 2000 holiday season. The fears of many never fully materialized. And yet, scores of businesses across America folded using September 11 as the reason they could no longer compete. Instead of admitting they had run their businesses poorly for some time, some business owners used a national tragedy as a scapegoat for their own shortcomings. I said in the original edition and and I reiterate here: *No one else is responsible for you making a profit.* Succeeding in business comes from you and the atmosphere you create within your own four walls.

Even the big boys are not as invincible as they once seemed. Kmart filed for bankruptcy December 2001. Their now ex-CEO's bold rescue plan was to be lower priced than Wal-Mart. He brought back the "Blue Light Special" and cut prices. With profit in decline, there was no money to update their antiquated inventory systems leaving their shelves empty of the best sellers and stocked with items that should have been marked down. At the same time, he cut back on his marketing budget which become virtually nonexistent during the holiday season. In short, he went to war without any ammunition. Once Wal-Mart learned of K-mart's plan, they simply lowered their prices in response. Being a much better run company, Wal-Mart could afford it. Kmart could not.

This again is a dramatic vindication of what we will explore in this book: *You can't win by continuing to cut prices or there will be no profit left to finance your ongoing operations.* Large or small, this is a lesson all businesses must heed.

Since this book was first published, I have presented seminars to thousands of owners and managers who are hungry for the tools to succeed. They leave excited to try their new sales tools but are met with skepticism at their stores. Owners encounter resistant managers and managers face reluctant owners. If you are resistant or reluctant, don't stand in their way. *Let those who enjoy the process work it.*

If you have an owner who doesn't want to change, decide if you can accept the futility of a dying enterprise. Likewise, if you have a store manager who is a critical naysayer, you need to decide if you can let them stay and wreck your business.

I myself have fired clients who slipped into mediocrity by not continuing to use the tools I gave them or who became complacent. Thinking they dodged the bullet and survived against a chain, *they returned to their old ways.*

But I also have many success stories that anyone can appreciate. In June of 2001, I was contacted by Trent Boaldin of Epic Touch to do an evaluation of his family's three electronics stores in the heartland of the country. When I arrived in Liberal, Kansas, the location of Dorothy's house from the Wizard of Oz, I stepped back in time to a town of 17,000 whose main industries were a stockyard, agriculture and oil.

The Boaldin family had created the Elkhart Phone Company in 1956. Since then this family had looked for ways to expand. They added a local PCS wireless network and when they needed a place for the hub servers, they rented two retail spaces in nearby Liberal, and Guyman. Since the servers took up little room, the family decided to use what remained to open two retail stores. They formed Epic Touch Communications to sell top-of-the line portable electronics. Sales had been dismal in the first year of operation. In addition they also purchased a Radio Shack store in Elkhart, population 2,500, which was holding its own but not growing.

After spending three days with Trent and his crews, I submitted a list of eighty-one recommendations to improve their operations based on my process outlined in this book. I returned in March of 2002 for a progress visit.

All eighty-one items had been checked off. The employees were helpful and knowledgeable. They were all using the five parts to a sale *exactly as I describe them in this book*. Their facilities had been upgraded, cleaned and remerchandised. Additional lighting had been added. POP signs were scattered throughout the stores. Merchandise that hadn't been selling had been donated to charity or sold at clearance. New displays and signage that featured their PCS wireless service had been added. Their marketing materials now featured a new name and tag line. They were tracking the daily sales of their stores, their departments and their salespeople. In short, they had taken ownership of making the business a success. Their phone service sales more than doubled and while their retail sales have not increased as quickly, all are certain they will.

This has all occurred since September 11, and in spite of a plunge in farm prices and a drought. These folks could have just given up. Instead, they took the time and courage to make huge changes in their business so when their economy picks up, they'll be ready.

I share this story because it shows how a small retailer followed my principles and made a big difference. The Boaldin family followed the path and it turned golden. They are a living example of the Kansas state motto: "Ad astra per aspera" *To the stars through difficulty.*

What we need in America are more pockets of businesses working at being the best. Families willing to risk. Employees eager to learn. That is how we will hold on to that unique feeling and respect for Main St., USA. That is how we hold on to the best that is America. But it does not come by expecting someone else to save you.

You are Bruce Willis or Sigourney Weaver in this action movie. Cast yourself as the one who will save your business. I am providing the tools and the encouragement to reclaim the greatness that is inherent in your business, but the actual work of succeeding falls squarely on your shoulders. And like Bruce Willis, it's an ongoing battle, one that never stops, just has sequels.

Good selling!
Bob Phibbs
01/15/03

Introduction

Your dad's hamburger stand, an institution for twenty years, is suddenly no longer packed. Old faces you used to see weekly haven't been by in a month. To you, it's a mystery; to them it's not.

Day in, day out you saw the same customers and families. You thought you had the best darn burger in town, and you did. But one day, Johnny Rockets opened a few doors down. Naturally, your regular customers went and tried it. What they found was an incredibly clean, though a bit too sanitized, well-lit fifties diner with a pleasant atmosphere. The food was not quite as good as yours, but they had a clever theme, good music and energetic employees. In that one visit, your customers made the comparison. They found you lacking, then told their friends to try the new place. You watched their lines grow and your business dwindle.

When chains move in, people are drawn to their familiar logo. Whether it is Johnny Rockets, Wal-Mart, Starbucks or GAP, a chain's biggest advantage over most independents is consistent standards. Customers know exactly what to expect: a known product, a clean environment and a familiar layout.

In order to compete you have to clean up your act, prepare your facility, train your salespeople to be personable and create an identity that is an integral part of your community. You can't just wait for the big guy to stumble so your customers come back to you. Big-boxes rarely trip up that bad.

In the 80s and 90s business boomed for many independent retailers. Though untrained in selling and marketing, loyal customers returned again and again because there really wasn't anywhere better to go.

Now those same retailers find themselves challenged by big-box stores that have opened just down the street. But these retailers don't know how to fight for customers; they never had to. Many have taken the easy way out and closed. That's not okay in my book.

You've Got Mail, the story of how Tom Hanks came in and put Meg Ryan's bookstore under, illustrates two major lessons.

Lesson #1—All the publicity in the world won't help unless you are willing to change the way you do business.

A Manhattan newspaper's feature story detailed her eminent demise. While I won't go into the incredible fortune she had at getting access to the writer, suffice it to say *that alone* was a big coup. Then the TV stations picked up the story. Meg had hung her star on public pity. But things at the bookstore didn't change.

Though her manager offered some suggestions for improving the quality of operations, she didn't listen. He went to work for the competitor and she closed down.

Lesson #2—If you are going to beat the drum about how unfair the chains are, you darn well better not be seen supporting one.

Think about it. Meg Ryan, the small independent business owner, sits in Starbucks and frets about being put out of business. See anything wrong with that? Yet many independent retailers won't bat an eye about shopping at any .com or big-box that can give them the lowest price. If you're not willing to support your neighbors, why should anyone support you?

Remember, everything being equal, when stores are equally stocked, equally priced and both have sufficient sales help, *people will buy where they have a relationship.* If things are unequal—maybe your store isn't the newest, maybe it's not near a freeway exit or maybe it's not the lowest priced—people will still buy from you if you have a relationship with them.

You made a commitment to your community when you opened

your shop. You opened your doors committed to offering a product or service that met the needs of your neighborhood. That community was good enough for you then, and it's good enough for you now.

Consumers want small neighborhood businesses like yours to succeed and if you pay attention to them, they will support you. If you are pushed to the wall, *you must change the way you do business because if you fail, it's your own fault.*

In December of '98 I was shopping in South Coast Plaza, singularly the highest grossing per square foot shopping center in the world. I had come to purchase two small handmade, hand-decorated chocolate gift boxes at one of the smallest shops you can imagine. I approached the counter, selected the items and as they were packaging them, I chatted with one of the workers. "You must really be doing well having been here so many years and with the economy so strong."

"Actually, we're closing at the end of the month," came the reply. I couldn't believe it. I asked to speak to the owner. She stepped up to talk with me.

"Yes, it's really sad, but everyone wants only Godiva chocolate."

"You're kidding!" I said.

"And rents are too high."

"Have you tried renegotiating the lease?"

"We've tried everything."

"How about selling from another location?"

"No, we can't move."

"Did you try to sell the business?"

"No, the recipes are ours and we don't want anyone else to have them."

I still couldn't believe my ears. I had just driven forty-five minutes out of my way in rush hour traffic to visit a specialty niche retailer in one of the world's premiere shopping destinations, and they were telling me everyone wanted Godiva! They had stubbornly decided they would change nothing! It was the holiday season;

consumer confidence was at an all time high, but they were going to go down with the ship.

What could the *Retail Doctor* have done for this little chocolate shop? PLENTY! Just for starters I'd:

- Get the owner away from the customers and hire a manager who believed in their unique product.
- Develop a website with point and click ways to personally design the chocolate boxes.
- Consider moving the store's kitchen to an industrial park where overhead would be lower.
- Hire an outside salesperson to sell the store as a source for personalized holiday gifts.
- Personally call on as many secretaries as possible with brochures touting the promotional aspect of the product, then repeat the fliers on a regular basis.
- Drop off a custom chocolate box with their company's logo and the CEO's name on it to the top 30 prospects.
- Find companies that do custom gifts and recognition awards and leave them similar samples.
- See if there was ever a customer list and then access it for a direct mailing that offers a free gift with purchase. If not, I'd start one immediately.

In short, there were *hundreds* of things that could have been done but weren't. The owners gave up on their customers and community relationship. One of my few regrets as the *Retail Doctor* was that I arrived at the scene to an already DOA client. I found a business owner who couldn't see the strength of their own product or any options to make their business work, a business owner who didn't have the tools to change course.

There are numerous articles about independents, nurseries, pharmacies, hardware stores or you-name-its going out of business. Most will quote the owner saying something like, *We can't compete. We're losing our customers to the chain stores. They get all the information and recommendations from us and then go to the chain store to buy at a discount.* Come on, do you believe this? Have independents actually had people say, *Thanks for the information. Now I'll go to Home Depot?*

While some retailers can cite anecdotal evidence, I can't imagine a majority of customers have responded that way. But when the occasional customer threatens to buy your product at a chain store, you need to be able to show them that while they think it is an apples to apples comparison, it is really apples to oranges. You have to have sales skills sharp enough to paint a picture of what services you include standard that a chain store doesn't. In short, you need to be able to sell yourself at a moment's notice.

> When the occasional customer threatens to buy your product at a chain store, you need to be able to show them that while they think it is an apples to apples comparison, it is really apples to oranges.

In addition, you must convince people that buying from an independent is vital to keeping Main St. alive. I was dealing with this very point one day at a hardware store when a salesperson asked, "What do we say to the person who says our prices are too high compared to Home Depot?" I quickly said, "I'd look the customer in the eye and say, 'I am holding on to a part of America with my independent store. I am working on a playing field that is grossly uneven. Nobody gave us tax credits to put our store in the community ten years ago. We are providing a fair product at a fair price; if you can support our efforts, great.'"

Are you going to make a buyer out of them? It could go either way, but at least you had a rebuttal. Can you tell your story effectively? Absolutely. Do people rally to stories? Yes. Will they remember you the next time? You bet.

But how can you give a stirring answer when you feel like you're about to go under? That's where I come in.

As the *Retail Doctor*, I give your business a complete examination. I look at what the owners have tried and then offer my frank analysis of what I see. I'm someone who'll tell you if you will live or die and give you the prescriptions to get you on your feet again. I show you the processes I use to make decisions so you can apply them to your own business.

But I'm only one doctor and even though I conduct a number of seminars each year, I can't reach everyone, so I've written this book. By purchasing it, you obviously are hoping to change your business, your attitude and your management style. And that is what I'm about, bringing hope back to independent businesses and giving them the tools to become and stay profitable.

CHAPTER 1

The Titanic and You
All Hands On Deck

Y ou are an independent retailer enjoying a steady, though not necessarily growing, business. On the other side of town, the centerpiece to the city's urban renewal, a new shopping center with a 30,000 square foot mega-chain store, is being built. You try not to think about it. You ask your suppliers how others faired when a category killer opened nearby. They assure you that, while business goes down a bit for a few months, it comes back within the first year. You brace yourself for a drop in sales of 10 percent. Within the first month business is off nearly 30 percent. You do the projections and calculate that at this rate, you will be gone before the end of the year; the following month sales are off 40 percent.

You accumulate debt so fast your profit and loss statement suddenly resembles that of a start-up. The mayor announces that a second mega-chain store is soon to open, this time within a mile of you. Though you hope you'll be fine; reality is, doom is on the horizon. You're taking on water and panic has set in. Your friends encourage you to contact the newspaper for a story about how you can't compete.

As an independent retailer, it is easy to feel hopeless in this situation. But I'm here to tell you: *You can compete*. Don't give up on your customers and your community, 'cause when the big chains fail —and some will have to—no one will be there to pick up the pieces.

If you are concerned enough to prevent your business from being another statistic, if independent business owner's tremendous pride (or *hubris)* can be squashed, if you heed indifferent customer warnings, you can keep your outcome from the fate of the Titanic.

The Titanic Story

She was an eleven-story wonder, watertight and invincible. On the fifth day of her voyage, the first warning came in, "Beware! Icebergs, growlers and field ice." It was ignored. An hour later, another report placed the ice 250 miles away, directly in her path. The captain remained unconcerned. Two more reports never reached him; he was busy entertaining his guests. Before turning in, he went to the bridge, saw the stars reflected in the smooth-as-stone sea and retired for the night.

Two more messages came in. Ice was dead ahead. The wireless operator, preoccupied with getting five days of messages off to the mainland, cut off the last ice warning from the ship, the *Californian*, saying, "Shut up, shut up. I'm busy."

An hour later, the ship received what appeared to be a glancing blow. There was no sense of shock or jar, just a single shudder. Although ice fell all over the deck, it seemed she had averted disaster. What they couldn't see was that the iceberg had ripped at the very heart of the ship below the water line. An hour later, she was gone.

Many look at the sinking of the Titanic as a loss of innocence and certainty. Much the same can be said for you, the independent businessman, who is seeing the quintessential American Dream ripped out from under you.

But don't lose hope just because you see icebergs all around you.

You can learn from the tragedy of the Titanic and heed her warnings.

How the Titanic Mirrors the Independent Business

The Titanic's crew thought that just because they hadn't seen the icebergs, they wouldn't collide with them. They were complacent. They had made voyages back and forth across the Atlantic. Ice in April was nothing unusual, and besides, they had a unique ship.

The independent retailer's temptation is to deny the threat of the chain store to their business and community. When they choose to do this, they find themselves in icy waters where countless nurseries, bookstores, furniture stores, craft stores, coffee houses, pharmacies, hardware stores and other lifebloods of the community have been sunk.

Important similarities exist between the Titanic disaster and the panicked small business owner:

- Seven reports were sent to the Titanic warning them of ice danger, yet the crew remained unmoved and in denial. Many retailers deny the threat of aggressive mega-chains. They think they'll be fine.

- The crew was untrained in handling messages; they filtered what they deemed important for the captain. In many retail establishments, communication between the owner and employees is often lax or unclear.

- The captain dined, appeared on the bridge and then slept. The big chain breaks ground. Signs appear, *Coming Soon*. The business owner takes in his normal Wednesday golf game.

- The crew didn't take the threat of sinking seriously. Many small retailers, no longer enjoying the struggle to survive, give employees control of the store with no direct consequences for wrong decisions.

- *Hubris* allowed the ship makers to feel invincible. Independent retailers, facing no competition and sure of their customer base, slip into mediocrity. Store interiors, once quaint, become dingy.

- The lookouts, couldn't even see the iceburgs until they were right on top of them, because the binoculars had been left in Southampton. Many businesses lack the tools to see disaster looming.

- The wireless operator was so concentrated on taking care of a bunch of frivolous messages, that he didn't take the seven ice messages seriously. With payroll, hiring, firing, and ordering, etc., many business owners get overwhelmed by having one more thing to think about.

- The Titanic had less than half the lifeboats necessary. Many independents have no strategy to survive the onslaught of mega-chains.

Many factors led to the Titanic's sinking just as many can lead to the demise of your business. If the builders and crew of the Titanic had had a clear vision of what could have been done to prevent her sinking, she might have made more than one crossing.

One final point. When the Titanic radioed her SOS, other ships came to the rescue. When one independent is threatened, other retailers must come to the rescue—full steam ahead.

CHAPTER 2

How We Got Here
and Who's to Blame

Originally, many independent retailers got into business because they saw an opportunity to fill a need in their community. If they had been driving for forty-five minutes to get to the closest hardware store, they decided their community could use such a store and committed themselves to filling that need. They worked their whole lives in retail, became the pulse of the community and passed on the legacy. Their shops gave people a reason to walk to multiple destinations. They created the city's heart and soul. Businesses existed for many years with the same customers. Whether business was good or bad, there was never a question that they would survive. After all, the community needed the independents' goods.

These same retailers now find themselves challenged by megachains and big-box stores. How do these predatory stores choose their locations? They find the place a successful independent discovered years ago and move in across the street or next door. The megachains know right where to settle.

But is the chain store, like the independent when he or she started, addressing a specific need for a product in the community? No. Big-box stores go into towns not to enhance their feeling of community but to provide maximum dividends for their shareholders. They want a community's entire shopping district reduced to their one-stop shop.

City council members and planning departments, anxious to do *anything* rather than the *right* thing, reward the biggest players and shut out the very business owners who made the town. The national chains get special tax incentives, redevelopment funds and sweetheart deals to come into a city—essentially they receive free stores. Yet the independent business owner, should they want to expand, must take a second mortgage on their house, becoming personally liable for the entire project. No such risk is there for the developer or the national chain. Their stock soars.

City planners say that it is a fundamental tenet for property owners to be able to do whatever they want with their holdings and that development is good. These *power centers* become virtually indistinguishable from every other one with their bland, poured concrete, tilt-up warehouses devoid of windows or paint. The town loses its unique shopping districts and its identity.

"I can't get deals like they get," is the frequent refrain of independent retailers. "They can sell it cheaper than I can buy it." They're right, but so what? Spending all your energy crying the blues doesn't help combat their massive buying power. You must find a way to add value to the customer's experience at your own store, and give them a compelling reason to return, rather than focusing on what you *can't* do.

Many independents hope to become the next Starbucks or McDonald's, cash out and then do what they *really* want, but they don't have the needed revenue and/or passion to build such an empire.

Consumers too have taken the easy way out. They are buying into the chain stores homogenization—from food to fashion, from furniture to books. These same consumers will tell you they like the image of Main Street but do not see the disconnect between patronizing a chain store and the wholesale destruction of their neighborhoods.

What Happens When the Going Gets Tough

What happens to your neighborhood when the big-box stores have gotten all their tax incentives and bought up the town? Is that when you bemoan the fact that there is nowhere *good* to shop? Will everyone be wearing GAP, drinking Starbucks and shopping Wal-Mart for everything from prescriptions to building supplies? If the big-box retailers all come in and the independents close shop, the consumer will have no other choice.

However, small businesses have a history in their community. If they enhance customer service with knowledgeable salespeople, upgrade their facility and create clever marketing, they are less at risk of being sunk by the big-box chains. If they give poor service or no service, then they have developed no relationship to hold on to their customers. They are inviting the chains into their neighborhood and are likely to sink.

CHAPTER 3

The More Things Remain the Same, the Less Likely Things Change

Ever see the cartoon Popeye? Every day for thirty years, Bluto captures Olive Oil, Popeye's girlfriend. He spirits her away and Popeye comes after him. Bluto, several feet taller and much stronger than Popeye, always beats him up. Then from out of nowhere a can of spinach appears. After eating the spinach, Popeye gains immense strength and exacts revenge. It is always the same.

Wouldn't it have been better if Bluto remembered before he tried to capture Olive Oil that he had never won this game? Couldn't he have found someone else to pick on first? And wouldn't it have been better if Popeye had eaten the spinach before he attacked Bluto?

To avoid disaster, look at holding on to existing customers *before* they have a chance to go elsewhere, instead of trying to get them to come back. It takes looking in the mirror at your strengths and leading with them, deciding what you can and are willing to change, and what you can't or don't want to change. You need to be *proactively* thinking about the results you want instead of *reacting* to the results you currently have. The veteran captain of the Titanic and many business owners share the belief that things will remain constant and therefore rarely make the necessary changes to avert disaster. If you continue to do these same things, you'll continue to get the same mediocre results.

You need to develop a plan, stick to it and realize you are adjusting the rudder on a big ship. A little change may not seem like much at first, but it will significantly alter your course. Left untreated, you may end up somewhere you hadn't intended to go.

Internal Motivation Comes from External Leverage

When the Titanic was just about to crash, the helm yelled to reverse engines and turn rudder. Faced with sufficiently deadly leverage the crew took evasive action, but it was too late to affect the outcome.

Leverage is an external circumstance that fundamentally challenges your survival. Leverage to a person with a drinking problem would be a doctor telling them, "You take one more drink and you'll die."

Leverage is not, *I want to be the next Starbucks.* Leverage is if we don't increase business by 15 percent, I won't be able to afford payroll. Leverage is something you have to look for on your own.

Look at the iceberg, the unstoppable chain store even before it gets near you. See the danger. Feel the fear of sinking and memorize it. Imagine your house foreclosed and your store vacant; try using that for leverage. Come up with whatever works to define failure for you. Every time you don't follow through with a change, remember clearly this leverage of the alternative. With that you can motivate yourself to action. Know *why* you need to alter the way you do business. See *what* circumstances might result from inaction. Motivate yourself to change *how* you do business to avoid your leveraged scenario.

I cannot motivate you to change. *No individual can motivate another to do anything.* Finding your inner motivation to change takes an honest appraisal of what *you* want to have as a result and getting the proper leverage on yourself to follow through.

The keys to your success include constantly upgrading your operation, training your employees better, building an alliance of other small businesses to pool your resources, and actively recruiting stellar management.

Reading this book will give you the tools to look out, not just to see the icebergs, but to alter your course before the chain stores rip a hole in your business and in your community.

CHAPTER 4

Look Around You
THE FACILITY

Now that we've met the icebergs and the people who created them, let's get down to how to survive in those icy waters. In order to survive, you need to make sure your own house is in order. Remember the Mary Tyler Moore show and her parties? They had a reputation for being bad. When guests arrived, there was Ted crooning off key at the piano or someone else having a fight or Mr. Grant taking too much veal Prince Orlaf. Something always went wrong. People just dreaded opening her door. When Johnny Carson arrived, all the lights went out. Mary understood why people didn't want to come but didn't know how to fix it.

For Mary Richards, all the sparkling and peppy invitations and assurances of fun didn't change the fact that her parties were always disasters. Likewise for an independent, all the advertising money and all the best sales training in the world cannot make up for a shoddy, unwelcoming environment.

Because environment is the first thing customers notice as they approach your door, I always begin my analysis with an evaluation of the facility. Here are some of the specific prescriptions I recommend.

Signs of the Times Are Not *Open*

In a major redevelopment not far from my house a Lone Star restaurant was under construction. For several months, a sign saying *Coming Soon* hung on the roof. Finally the restaurant sported a *Now Open* banner. A few people tried it, but not many came back. One month later the banner came down and was replaced with a massive red logoed sign. Still, the place wasn't busy. Maybe the management of the chain, reacting at the lack of business thought, "Hmm, they must not think we're open." So they mistakenly tacked on a small, cheap, red neon OPEN sign. With a little creativity, they could have added an animated neon longhorn sign that would have piqued our interest rather than just state the obvious. Of course, the real point they needed to address was *why* people hadn't come back.

The Myth of Marketing: If you spend it they will come. All the advertising money and all the best sales training in the world cannot make up for a shoddy, unwelcoming environment.

When it comes to your facility, don't confuse something with the *right* thing.

The end of the 90s saw a proliferation of OPEN signs in the windows of fast food chains, so people could quickly see they were open all night. For those late night fast food places, it was a good idea—but just for them.

Many independents, thinking an OPEN sign will add *something*, tack it onto their front window and wait for the money to roll in, regardless of whether the sign goes with anything else in their store's concept or overall look. Many leave them on the same circuit as their security lights so even when they are closed, they're OPEN. How's that for attention to detail?

If you really need a cheap neon look-alike sign to tell the public you are open for business, that is the least of your problems. If your store is too dark to tell if it is open, add lights. If your store windows have tinted film, get rid of it. But please don't think an OPEN sign will pack people in.

Do You See What I See?

Have you driven by your store and considered what the average person who knows nothing about your business sees? Does the ambiance of the inside begin on the outside? Is it clean and presentable?

Make sure we can clearly see your logoed sign. If we can't, trim trees to improve site lines. If bulbs are burnt out, replace them. Every morning sweep off the sidewalks and pick up trash in your parking lot. Empty your trashcans. If you have benches out front, keep them inviting and sturdy. Add some potted plants to your doorway. If your front door gets dinged every day, then for the cost of a can of paint, paint it.

Monitor your establishment throughout the day for handprints on windows, overflowing trashcans and trash by your front door. If you have a spot for planters, make sure you have pretty flowers growing.

Don't expect the city or mall to provide the ambiance for your store. If you're on a dark street, add lights from your interior to light up the sidewalk in front of your business. If your mall skylights are dark at night, do the same thing. You must be the brightest business on the block, not only in intellect, but also in allure.

If you have a patio, add mood lighting so it has its own ambiance. Party lights, subtle halogen lights and Christmas lights are all choices that set a mood encouraging customers to linger—without an OPEN sign.

Finally, cigarette-smoking employees out in front of your store keep shoppers away. They broadcast to the world *there's nothing going on inside. I'm bored and I know you will be too.* Don't allow anyone, on the clock or off, to detract from your business.

People Attract People—Make Sure They Can See In

Can people see into your store? If not, you're losing out on one of the basic tenets of retail: *people attract people*. Great windows make passersby stop and wonder, *what's going on in there?* Windows that are cluttered, covered, over-signed or dirty create obstacles to people taking more than a passing interest in your shop. Clean those windows off!

I always seem to be in a client's store during the holidays when window painters come asking if the owner wants their windows painted with snowmen. I always say, "NO!" In December *especially*, people are window shopping. Anything that impedes a person's ability to quickly look in at a busy store is bad for business.

When a store is empty, it is much harder for that first person to walk in; they feel all eyes are on them. Get your employees out from behind the counter and keep them active. Customers outside need to see people inside trying on clothes, matching prints, perusing books, comparing products, doing something as if they were customers. Activity draws the window shopper in.

Some of the larger big-box stores stack merchandise against their front windows. For them, the idea of window dressing went out the window a long time ago, and I suspect, impulse sidewalk shopping went down significantly. Could an independent retailer capitalize on this weakness? You bet!

Put Something in that Window!

A great window tells one story and tells it well. It serves as an invitation to the passerby. A well-designed window display encourages impulse sales and peaks a customer's curiosity. It might even tug at their heartstrings.

A June display at a jewelry store featured a miniature park scene. Seated on one end of an oak bench, a young woman held out her left hand as her fiancé on bended knee, placed a sparkling platinum diamond ring on her finger. At the other end of the bench, an elderly woman, alone, admired her own wedding band. A simple sign overhead said, "A diamond is forever."

A window's message must be clear, its point of view obvious and its merchandise fully accessorized. That means if you have a great Hawaiian shirt (hopefully the most expensive in the store) make sure you put sandals, belt, shorts, puka shells, straw hat, sunglasses and a fan, umbrella or volleyball with it. Add tickets and it's a travel agency, add a picnic basket and you're a gourmet deli, add a boom box and you're an electronics store. Whatever you choose to emphasize, make sure it tells a complete story and is well lit. Work with other independents to feature their merchandise in your windows and vice versa.

Display the Whole Picture

Ever see what happens to both children and adults when you put a train set on display? They stand mesmerized, watching as it chugs around the eight-foot circle. At the same time they notice everything it passes including your barbecue set, your dishtowels, fishing gear or even your western wear.

Just like with your windows, you want customers to notice more than just one item in a display. Make sure the relationships are obvious. If you feature a BBQ, make sure you have the utensils, citronella candles, aprons, charcoal, OFF spray and picnic baskets. If you carry the western shirt in both women's and men's sizes, make sure you feature them together. The men's will sell the women's and the women's the men's—especially since married women tend to do most of the dressing of their husbands. We don't want to see just a display of apples and spices, but all the fixin's to make a pie. We don't want to see just the dress, jacket and purse, but the scarf that picks up the jacket's subtle color, the earrings that match the dress and the shoes that make it an outfit.

Lighten Up! People Don't Shop Where It's Dark

To every retailer I work with, I always suggest adding more lights. Bright and cheery stores are inviting. Colors look better and energy levels are higher. Due to the energy crisis in the mid-seventies, stores were given a fixed wattage per square foot for total lighting. The designer/builder divided the wattage between fluorescents and floodlights. Stores ended up lit by formula rather than by need. Either nothing stood out because it was so dim, or nothing stood out because it was all too bright. The best selling environments balance darker and lighter areas.

Consider what you're lighting and then create the environment you want to highlight. For example, if you have a large winter display of sweaters, wool shirts and outerwear, create the warm atmosphere of a cozy cabin. Add small lamps in glowing shades of yellow and red and you're halfway there. A similar mood would also sell outdoor sporting books, fireplace equipment or pipes and tobacco. If you are showing what's new at the beach, concentrate spotlights from the ceiling.

Good lighting makes merchandise pop. Create new areas of interest with single lights focused on no more than a two-foot wide circle. Create a new ambiance with table lamps that draw our attention and add warmth to the area. Consider mixing in some spotlights to highlight displays and counter areas. Always check that they do not shine directly in anyone's eyes. Small halogen bulbs are excellent for lighting colorful items as well as for pinpointing smaller goods. Consider getting the screw-in types that do not need specialized fixtures and are easy to maintain. Replace your old 150-watt floodlights with the newer halogen 90-watt spots.

You may be able to double your lighting instruments without adding more circuits. If you can't, hire an electrician and add a circuit or two. Double-check your light fixtures for wattage requirements. It's not a question of expensive designer fixtures, just adding light.

The only exception I've found was at Illuminations, a beautiful candle store, in Old Towne Pasadena. At night they are lit only by candles—lots of candles to be sure, but a big open front window lets everyone look in and see the people and their products—brilliant!

The Retail Doctor's Ten Steps to Merchandising

- At least once a month change your displays. Holidays and seasons only last so long and promotional goods have a short shelf life. See what you have to work with. Display new arrivals first. Remember if you ordered merchandise meant to go together, keep it together. You don't want its first appearance to be diluted. Later, the few items that may be left can be grouped with new arrivals to give them a new look. If you ordered holiday candles from one vendor, mugs from another, and teas from another, remember and wait for them all to arrive. Don't put the candles out first as a sole item and lose the potential add-on sale. (Just a reminder, it always helps to take a digital camera on any buying trip).

- Choose the products to merchandise. Don't choose the things the customer already needs; those are what they are coming in for. A customer responds to things they want. So don't display the cheap hand mixer when the fancy KitchenAid is what every *Emeril* wannabe desires. Just because all they really *need* is a mixer, doesn't mean they won't treat themselves to the expensive model if it is displayed prominently.

- Look for *one thing* that makes a group. All of one product works well in a grocery store, but it is little more than warehousing the items in a retail store. Consider displaying by product *use*—all items related to brewing and drinking tea for example. Consider displaying by color—the strongest color combinations to attract attention in retail are red, white and black. Consider related or contrasting colors. Just a reminder, our eyes tend to quickly get the point and move on, so never make a monochromatic display.

- Start with the display area closest to the front door and put your newest and most expensive items in the spotlight. If security is a concern, find a way to protect your products from shoplifters. Be sure to have several levels of height and enough products so that the customer can pick up and touch without having to totally dismantle your display. Don't ever put up a sign that says DO NOT TOUCH even in a glass store. You might as well put up a sign that says DO NOT BUY.

Displays are *supposed* to get messed up. That means people have looked at your merchandise. That is a good thing.

- Find a totally unrelated item and put it in your display. It serves as a prop, its only purpose to grab your customer's attention. Add a stuffed toy pig to complete your Kitchenaid display. It is not necessary to add a prop to every display, but the idea should always be there.

- Light your display like it's showtime. Adjust overhead lighting. If you have a particularly dark display and no way to highlight it from above, consider moving it to an existing light source or light it from below with small spot lights. Remember, light makes the merchandise *pop*.

- Add a few well-placed, well-worded signs. Make sure they are short and easy to read. If your customers are mostly seniors, make it easy on them by using larger fonts. Handwritten signs with markers are okay for a kid's lemonade stand, but anywhere else they tend to look amateurish.

- Move existing displays around in the store when new merchandise comes in. Since the fairly new products will still be selling, switch your displays two weeks after their arrival. Move one display from the front to the middle of the store and the other from the middle to the back, rather than recreating everything every time. For example, don't dismantle the swimsuit display when fall merchandise arrives in July, just create the fall display at the front and move the swimsuits to the middle of the store.

- Monitor your computer printouts and inventory levels weekly. If something really takes off, be prepared to reorder immediately. If you have sold through your inventory and you have no back-stock, change the display out to something you have plenty of. If something doesn't sell, try moving the same display to another location before giving up on it.

- Finally, make sure all of your stock is priced; if it's not, *price it.* No one wants to have to ask how much something is.

Discover the Aspects of Movement

Customers are funny; they like things in the same place, but they also like to be surprised. Since 80 percent of your business comes from 20 percent of the people you see in a day, you must move everything around to keep it fresh.

Howard & Phil's Western Wear store in South Coast Plaza was in trouble when I was brought in. The message I wanted to send immediately was that things were going to be different. I descended on that store like a whirlwind. For five hours all I did was move things. I moved racks into the *safe zone,* that area most retailers mistakenly use as a buffer between the store and the mall or the store and the street. No longer could people size up the store quickly and then walkout. Doing that created a place for the customer to browse the newest, most exciting merchandise.

To lead them invitingly into the rest of the store, I created little areas of discovery.

I angled four-way racks at forty-five degrees to create new traffic patterns. I graduated the racks' heights, getting taller towards the back of the store. The big rounders that held pants were moved near the walls to allow as much space and flow as possible and to open up the center of the store.

Then I moved the merchandise, filling the racks with an eye to color and brightness. I created three main display areas. At the entrance I focused on only three colors: red, white and black. Twenty feet in on both sides were displays that also used red, white and black but that held different merchandise. Finally, the back section displays picked up just the red and the white.

I concentrated the *wants*, impulse items customers *didn't* come in for, to the entrance of each section. I loaded the rounders with the *needs*, things they came in specifically to buy, at the back of the store. A typical four-way held the latest jeans and a new print shirt. On the crosspiece, I placed a Tony Lama boot on top of its box. On the other side, I created a similar women's four-way but with denim skirts, an embroidered top and a new Justin boot atop its box.

On the boot walls that surrounded the store, I placed all of the most exotic, high priced boots at eye level.

I moved the old sale merchandise that had been featured in the front to one well-marked rounder in the back. Customers now had to move through the store to find it.

Everything was cleaned and dusted; everything was priced. There was a new sweep to the store—and all of this had occurred while we were open.

Of course, you have to train your salespeople on what to say after you've moved everything in your store around. Customers are going to find things once hidden and think they are new. The following is a question your staff might hear and three letter grades of answers. A customer admires a shirt "Oh, did you just get this in?" he asks.

Failing answer: "No, we've had that for a long time." Message the customer hears is *only the most recent arrival is worth buying*.

D answer: "I don't know." Message to customer is *you bore me, don't bother me, not my job*.

A answer, the only right answer: "Yes, doesn't it look great?" Message to customer is *your choice is great and that's all that really matters*. While the exact wording can vary, the intent is the same; it is new to the customer and they like it.

Many retailers are fearful their customers won't like change so they keep things the same, but the evidence is overwhelming that customers *enjoy* change. With all this movement at Howard & Phil's, people who came in for their *needs* picked up a lot of *wants,* resulting in the highest sales increase for that month among their fifty stores.

People need to discover what you have. The best stores know this and create little unexpected areas. Contrast this to the big-box retailers who have no mystery, only regimented departments laid out in straight lines. They force the traffic in predetermined areas, robbing customers of retail's element of discovery. Think a tire store, a milk case in a grocery store, an underwear display. Now think an antique store, a fancy soap store or a gourmet deli. How do each of them present their merchandise?

The independent retailer has a personal connection with their customers and they have filled their stores with *wants*. The biggest danger for small retailers is what they do with these wonderful *wants*. If they treat them as needs, nothing stands out. *Wants* and *needs* are not interchangeable. Don't stack up these profitable treasures in unremarkable settings like a large chain store. They will just sit there until you finally put them on sale.

> Keep things moving and you can avoid markdowns and increase customer interest.

Don't Forget the Holidays!

There are at least two great holiday opportunities for changing the ambiance of the store, Christmas and the 4th of July. Ambiance has nothing to do with product or displays. The walls at Polly's Gourmet Coffee in Long Beach, CA are a natural cedar that has darkened with age. The wood gives an old time feel to the store, as if it has existed for a hundred years. During the summer, this rustic ambiance lends itself to displays of bright flags and patriotic colors that wake up the interior. From November to the first week of January, the walls are covered with dried grapevines strung with multi-colored lights. These changes give an overall festive feel to the store, a perfect backdrop in which to display merchandise. The customer quickly senses the themes and their interest in buying is unconsciously heightened.

All retailers must change their stores shopping environment often. Every holiday season or theme lends itself to something. Remember that most customers see your store several times during the year. It is always best to change its ambiance before they get bored.

Change Your Register Signs

The last thing a customer sees is your register area. It is their last impression of what kind of operation you have. I always suggest replacing the big sign that screams NO REFUNDS, NO RETURNS. These have to be the most offensive items in a store and the ones that owners seem to feel will protect them from the hordes of customers who are waiting to take advantage of them. Nothing could be further from the truth. First, anyone who pays by credit card MUST get a refund—in most states it's a law. If you deny the credit card holder a refund, all they have to do is write to their card issuer and deny the charge. Why would you want to make anyone go through such an ordeal? Second, why is it okay to take a customer's money and not give it back? Are you that unsure of the quality of your goods? While I understand that your return policy may have a time limit or that customers may try to return clothing after they've worn it, there is a better way to enforce your policy than a sign screaming at them from behind your counter. Have it on your receipts or as an additional small piece of paper you attach to a receipt if it really is a problem. Even then, if a customer is that unhappy, I always recommend just giving their money back. It is simply not worth the aggravation to you or them. Plus, if they don't get their way, they'll tell everyone how unfair you are.

Any sign that starts with no is a barrier to the relationship you've hopefully just made in your store. There are many ways to deal proactively with genuine concerns. Think how you would want to be treated.

It Really Is the Little Things

I know this section may have seemed to state the obvious but we have to start with the basics. Is your store clean? Is it well lit? Is it easy to see from front to back? Can you see all the customers, or do high racks hide them? Are the displays interesting and changed often? If so, you are following the basic principles to success.

When the owner is distracted, the facility deteriorates, and this is the first unheeded warning at the entrance to icy waters. Consider splitting your store into sections and assigning people to keep everything looking shipshape. Make sure you monitor their assignments and you'll find you have to do less while achieving more.

Have a vision, make a plan and your facilities and displays will move your merchandise. Merchandise your store like your life depends on it. It does.

CHAPTER 5

Sell Like You Know Them
THE BASICS OF SALES

Many independents have adopted the model of the chains. They have cut down on employees, given up on sales training and stockpiled merchandise. They falsely believe their products will sell themselves. Nothing could be further from the truth.

In these times of cost cutting and technology, most retailers have given up on hiring salespeople and instead have settled for hiring cashiers. They have undercut the competitive advantage the independent has, passionate salespeople.

Say sales and we think used cars and door-to-door vacuums. Most people think all salespeople are *Willie Lomans*, despicable losers out to push unwanted products on an unsuspecting and gullible public.

I'll never forget peeking into the sales manager's office of a car dealership in Long Beach and seeing an engraved Sucker of the Month plaque complete with picture.

> A product doesn't sell itself; it takes a salesperson.

That month's winner was a smiling grandmother standing in front of her new Ford.
Seeing that Polaroid taped to the center of
the plaque represented all that is bad in sales.
To think that every month those salesmen
are laughing behind someone's back lends
credence to the acknowledged wariness that
the public holds for anyone in the field of
sales. A good sales force doesn't make suckers
out of their customers, they make friends.

> Nothing can take the place of that transference of feeling, not marketing, not location and certainly not cashiers.

Selling is something we all do every day.
Look around you. You've made plans to go out with friends on
Friday night. Someone chooses the restaurant and convinces everyone else to go. That's selling! Before you go out that night, the dry
cleaning must be collected. Somehow you convince your partner to
do it. That's selling! How did you end up at the foreign film when
your choice was Woody Allen? You acquiesced after being told key
elements of the story that resonated within you. Afterwards at the
local ice cream shop, you were glad you did. The next morning over
coffee at the independent coffeehouse, you sell the film to a friend.
The cycle continues, one salesfriend to another.

Selling is nothing more than a transference of feeling. If I feel
good about a product or service, I transfer that feeling to everyone I
meet. Likewise, if I don't feel good about a product, a service, my job
or myself, I pass on that feeling as well.

Customers will return to shop where they've made a relationship.
They can't do that at a Home Depot that has lots of merchandise but
no salespeople. That wasn't always the case with large retailers.

When I moved to Long Beach twenty years ago, I needed curtains. I went to J.C. Penney's where an elderly lady came over and
asked if I needed help. Instead of just pointing me to the ready-
mades, she took the time to ask the right questions. When she realized I knew nothing about my windows, she politely and carefully

showed me how to measure them. Next she showed me some of the products they had. I thanked her, returned home and came back with the measurements. She continued to guide my choices. Afterwards, I went to the management office to offer my compliments. The manager said, "Oh yes, she's been cited many times over the years for her excellent customer service."

Go into a Penney's now and you are likely to meet no one. Their few cashiers have little product knowledge or interest in helping people. Department store clerks in general appear to be only one step up from convenience store cashiers. Yet, J.C. Penney's was built on service. With their stock plummeting 80 percent beginning in 1998, the president of the company made the bold announcement that Penney's needed more name brands at lower prices to increase sales. Wow, what a bold idea! But a year later, with sales still plummeting, they followed up with a $200 million ad campaign. What they should have announced was an increase in knowledgeable salespeople to get back to their roots of great customer service.

In most large retailer stores, if you have a question about an item, no one knows more than you do and all you know is what you can read off the cardboard package. No one is there to offer suggestions. No one has used the product themselves. No one can give you a tip on how to use it.

The employee may know that their new shirt is expensive, but they don't know how to justify its cost. They don't know that it's made from a special fiber that keeps it from wrinkling. A lack of service due to a lack of knowledge, that is what we expect from a big-box retailer. The advantage belongs to the well-trained sales force of the independent.

While pretending to shop for a BBQ at Sun West True Value in Arizona, I was shocked when the salesman, while pointing out the features of their best BBQ, told me Home Depot carried it for $20 less. I thought, "Why is he bringing up the big-box retailer and telling me the better deal was there?" Before I could finish my thought, he continued, "But of course, they charge you $20 for delivery, and you have to put it together yourself. We can deliver it put together. Within the hour you'll be cooking on it." That was an excellent way to address the big-box. He acknowledged that Home Depot appeared to have a better price but sold me on why buying from him would be better for me. The price of an item can be justified if you have a knowledgeable salesperson.

All things being equal, if a chain store and an independent have the same widget at the same price, the customer will buy from the independent they have a relationship with. Further, if they both have the same widget and the independent's is priced higher, the customer will still buy there if salespeople understand it's not just price that leads customers to buy. Salespeople make sure comparison shopping is always apples to oranges—never apples to apples. You have something unique that makes you the better choice and it's not product. Your ability to share that knowledge with a customer builds the relationship that independents thrive on.

It's Not the Words, It's the *Intent*

The intent a salesperson brings to a sale opens a window that either exceeds a customer's needs or slams it shut in their face. For example, a couple walks in to an independent nursery looking for something to plant. They ask the employee what type of palm tree to put by their pool. He says with a *you jerk* attitude, "You can't put a palm tree by a pool. They are just too dirty!"

"Then what can we plant?"

"Pool plants are over there." He points, turns and leaves.

The wife says, "That was rude and he doesn't know any more than we do." Ten seconds later they're in their car headed for the big-box.

As the employee heads for the next customer he thinks, "Boy, do I get the stupid ones."

What he didn't hear was that they didn't necessarily want a palm tree; what they wanted was something tall to accent their pool. The

Day after day, employees who treat customers with derision are squandering the independent's competitive advantage. And why? Because most of them grew up in a *Married With Children* world where even the four year old has a snide comment about their own mother. Young people have rarely seen good sales models or customer service. Customer service in many businesses is based on McDonald's— whether the customer received their "Big Mac" in under 30 seconds.

customers took his attitude as a lack of knowledge, but his intent on being right precluded any further questions and lost him the sale.

What if in that scenario, the employee had started with, "A palm tree wouldn't be my first choice because they're so dirty. Is there a particular reason you want one?"

The customer might say, "Cause that's all I've seen. What else is there?"

The salesman says, "We have all sorts of plants to add height and interest in addition to our large assortment of palms. May I show you a few?"

What's the difference? The intent of the salesperson. One says what you can and can't do; the other asks what you are trying to accomplish. The proper intent invites us to feel that we are listened to.

The day I took over management of Howard & Phil's at South Coast Plaza, a customer asked for black boots. The salesperson quickly pointed to the shelf and showed them the only three styles he had and said, "That's it, they just don't go with much." The dissatisfied customer left without even trying them on.

I immediately taught the crew that even though they probably knew the customer would never buy the black boots, there was a way to make those sales. "Never show just products the customer asks for," I said. "Selling is a game. You know they probably aren't going to buy the black boots. You have to guide them through making that decision on their own and that means getting a pair of black boots on them as quickly as possible. You need to have some of your best sellers in their size ready to try on. Once they see the color on their feet, most times they decide they don't like the look."

Often the customer would buy another color. Some employees would say I made the customer buy something they didn't want. I answered, "No, I gave them a chance to see they didn't necessarily want black. I showed them other options, and they left with a new pair of boots. Just what they came in for."

Remember that it is not your employees' job as salespeople to show only what a customer asks for, especially when other options are available and better. It *is* their job to always find a way to get the sale. It takes training. It takes practice. It takes creativity. It takes knowing the five parts to a sale.

You Must Know and Teach the Five Parts to a Sale

A sale is the orderly process of developing a relationship and matching your product with the customer. As long as you understand the fundamentals, it is much like a movie. We need to meet the characters, find out what motivates them, find out their conflict or need, build to a climax, offer a resolution and end happily. It's the same in sales.

The salesperson greets the customer, finds out what brought them there, matches up their needs with products and then clinches the sale. The customer pays for it and walks out happily.

Training your employees on the five parts to a sale shows them that there is an orderly process to building rapport, developing a relationship and making a sale. And remember: selling is nothing more than transferring your positive feelings to your customers.

THE FIVE PARTS TO A SALE

1. Greeting—Welcome to My Place… with a Prop

You need to greet your customers as if they are friends arriving at your home with *Welcome*. Without that, there is no foundation on which to build a relationship. Further, you need to modify the energy of your greeting depending on who you are talking with.

Because customers walk in with differing energy levels, you need to be able to sense their level of energy and adjust yours accordingly. Out of 180 stores in the mall, they've chosen yours as the first of only three they will visit. When they connect with your salesperson, three things can happen:

1. The salesperson has 250 watts of energy and is so hyper and excited the customer thinks they are on some kind of drug and leaves.

2. The salesperson has 25 watts of energy and is so depressing and bored that the customer immediately senses it and leaves. This is the norm for many struggling businesses.

3. The salesperson matches the customer's energy level and adds a bit when they connect with the merchandise. The customer begins to shop.

We want number three. Your salesperson must always be plugged in, full of energy.

However, the untrained salesperson typically asks, "Can I help you find something?" The customer answers *No* and thinks, *Why can't they just let me look?* The salesperson wonders why he ever bothered to ask in the first place when everyone always says no. Nothing draws them

> The quickest way to thwart the building of rapport and the development of a relationship is to use the words, *Can I help you find something?* These are absolutely the worst words to greet any customer with and are never acceptable.

together with this meaningless question. It serves as an exit for both the customer and the salesperson. Both end up feeling worse than before they met—two people with no relationship, uncomfortable with the shopping experience. Yet this ritual has become the norm and is why sales have decreased for many retailers. To stand out from the masses, acknowledge every customer with a smile within fifteen seconds of their entrance. Stop whatever you are doing and give the customer your undivided attention. That means if you are on the phone, ask them to hold. If you are talking to another employee, stop mid-sentence. If you are with another customer say, "Please excuse me while I greet the person who just walked in."

The best way to greet a customer is to put a prop in your hand, get out from behind the counter and walk over to them. If you are a hardware store, your prop might be some tool; if you are a clothing store, it might be a shirt; if you are a nursery, it might be a small plant. The prop makes you appear busy and yet willing to interrupt what you are doing to put your customer at ease. At the same time, it gives you an opportunity to say hello.

Next, make sure you get their eye, and say something fairly well scripted. I always like, "Welcome to (your store name). Take a look around, if you have any questions, I'll be right back." And with that, leave the customer and get rid of your prop. Casually monitor what they are looking at. After a few minutes return to them and continue with the second part of the sale.

You have something unique that makes you the better choice and it's not product. Your ability to share that knowledge with a customer builds the relationship that independents thrive on.

2. Windows of Contact—Compliment, Share and Continue

The second part of the sale builds rapport with a customer by using what I call **Windows of Contact**. During this part you want to show them that you are a real person, that you are worth talking to.

You want to get them from *Oh my God, a salesman* to *Oh wow, this is a nice person*. You want to find something in common and build a conversation from that exchange; you want to be their friend.

Compliment. When a customer walks into your store, take a moment to size them up. Notice what they are wearing, what their expression is or what they are carrying. Then see if you can begin a conversation based on one of those things. For example, a middle-aged woman walks into your coffeehouse with two small kids in tow. She is a bit rattled, and she is wearing a *Soccer Mom* T-shirt. As she approaches the counter, a conversation might begin like this, "Welcome to Bob's Java. Looks like you have your hands full. Did you just come from practice or a game?"

"Oh no! Thank God, soccer ended last month."

Share. "Yeah, when both my niece and nephew were playing soccer; my sister-in-law was really run ragged. They were in two different leagues, both playing on the same day in two different parks."

She smiles and says, "I'm glad that's not the case with me."

Continue. "Yeah, me too." You smile and ask, "What can I make for you today?"

Contrast that to the soccer mom who enters and you immediately ask, "How can I help you?" She is put on the defensive. You have given her no time to look around, to decompress from driving in with the kids or to get comfortable with her surroundings. You have pressured her to decide quickly because you make it seem like you're in a hurry to make the sale and get her out of there. No conversation ensues—you have become the chain store.

But because you are not Starbucks, you don't have the national brand recognition to bring them back. Don't despair, the relationships you develop by opening **Windows of Contact** will bring them back again and again.

What if a guy walked into your store with a USC sweatshirt on, and you knew the big game was that weekend. Could you find the way to open a window? Sure. You'd say, "Are you lucky enough to be going to the game?" **Compliment**.

"No, but I wish I was."

"Me too, but a beer and the TV will have to do. **Share**. What can I make for you today?" **Continue**.

With both the soccer mom and the USC guy, you didn't just state the obvious. You asked a question that took what you noticed and personally connected it to your own experience and came up with a conversation builder.

An even easier way to open a **Window of Contact** is to give a genuine compliment on a customer's jewelry or clothing. Nobody ever closes the window on sincere flattery. At South Coast Plaza, women often came in dressed to the nines. I found it easy to strike up conversations by complimenting them on their outstanding choice of jewelry. "Wow," I once began, looking at a huge amethyst stone on a sterling silver chain around an otherwise unremarkable woman. "That is a fabulous pendant. Did you design it yourself?" She smiled and said, "Yes, I found the amethyst on our trip to the Bahamas." Windows open for me to share? Gems, traveling and the Bahamas.

Another time a woman came in with a stunning emerald ring. When I asked her the same question, she said she didn't design it herself but added, "My husband had it designed by our favorite jeweler for our fifteenth anniversary." Windows open? Jewelry and relationships. Either way, it was up to me to build on those compliments and blend in a piece of my own experience with jewelry or traveling rather than just asking them more questions about their ring or pendant.

I am not saying lie to customers. If something is garish or ugly don't say it looks great—people can sense you are being insincere or sarcastic and will avoid you from then on.

If nothing stands out when you size them up initially, you can always open the window with the old standbys, work and weather but they are much weaker.

However, the window never opens when you state the obvious;

in fact it can sound stupid. For example, a stupid question for Soccer Mom would have been, *Do your kids play soccer?* and for the USC fan, *Do you like USC?*

Learning how to ask the right questions to open **Windows of Contact** takes time, especially for beginning salespeople like teenagers. As a manager, when you hear a salesperson asking seemingly stupid questions, take them aside afterwards in private and ask them if they noticed the silence from the customer. Hopefully they'll respond yes and if they don't, tell them that you noticed. Ask them what other questions they could have asked to open a conversation more easily and role play what they would share about themselves before they continued. Your goal during the first two steps of the sale is to build trust before pitching your wares.

3. The One Qualifying Question

The follow up to **Windows of Contact** is to qualify the person standing in front of you as a customer and continue to develop rapport. *What can I make for you today?* is a fine start for a coffee house. *What's your project?* is great for a hardware, craft or hobby store. At this stage of a sale you want to LISTEN and gather information. You don't want to ask twenty close-ended questions because that is not how we speak; it is how police interrogate.

Open-ended questions are always used to get the customer to tell you something. If a customer comes in looking for a gift, ask, "Could you describe him/her to me?" If they are looking for blinds, ask, "What does your existing furniture and room look like?" If they are looking for a coffee gift, ask, "What kind of coffee drinker is she?" After you've developed a rapport using **Windows of Contact**, these open-ended questions help give you information and pull you into the sale.

If you see someone picking up several white blouses, it would be safe to assume they are looking for a white blouse. Don't ask the lame closed-ended question, "Are you finding everything okay?" And don't ask the stupid question, "Are you looking for a white blouse?" Instead, take the initiative and ask the open-ended question, "You know, I have a few more white blouses over here that we just got in. Do you like cotton or maybe silk?" That exchange shows your intent is to truly help the customer and continues building your rapport.

Qualifying a customer is just asking the right questions. But do not come right out and ask people what they want because order takers do not get additional sales. You either take note of what they are looking at, comment on similar items or show them other locations where you have the same item.

But you can't do that until you have first developed rapport and made the customer a friend.

4. Features and Benefits

After you have an idea of the customer's needs, you must point out a specific feature of your product and then tell the customer how that feature will benefit them. A feature starts with *it has* and a benefit continues with *so you.*

I teach features and benefits by having the new hires go out to a busy corner. I have them point up at the sky for twenty seconds. We then go back to the meeting room and I ask the group, "What did people driving or walking past do when they saw what we were doing?" The response is always that the passersby looked up.

"And what did they see?"

"Nothing."

"And what did they feel when they saw nothing?"

"Stupid."

So it is with features and benefits. If you can only point out features, you are just pointing at the sky, which turns customers off because you didn't tell them why it was important. If a car dealer only said, "This coupe has a thirty-six-valve engine with dual overhead camshafts," you'd probably be lost. If he doesn't tell you why thirty six-valves are important, he makes you feel stupid and any rapport you might have had is lost.

Likewise, you can't just point out the benefit if you don't refer it back to a specific feature. If that same dealer had said, "Buy this coupe and you can zoom out of here and not change your oil for 100,000 miles. And it gets great gas mileage!" You'd wonder what made him make those claims. Benefits are only half of the equation; you must also tell them why.

Consider if the car dealer had said, "This coupe has a thirty-six-valve engine with dual overhead camshafts, so you get more horsepower with less gas and less maintenance." Suddenly you're listening. Features and benefits is a package deal and can't be split up.

When you point out a feature, think of the customer asking, "Why are they telling this to me?" Then you just answer their question with a benefit. Remember, features begin with *it has*; benefits start with *so you*.

If a customer asks what's so great about a shirt, you might say, "It has a pen hole through the pocket top (feature you picked out) so you can slide your pen in and out without having to lift the flap on the pocket (benefit to the customer)." It always has to be a feature and a benefit.

This is so simple, and I don't know why it is such a hard concept for new employees to grasp. Pick anything in front of you right now. Give me a feature. A window has tinted glass. The couch has overstuffed arms. The pen has a ballpoint.

Now match up what you saw with a benefit for each one. This window has tinted glass so you can save on air-conditioning. This couch has overstuffed arms so you can relax with your legs over them. This pen has a ballpoint so you can write better on more kinds of paper.

Everything has a feature and a benefit no matter how obvious it may seem. You would never buy anything unless you saw a benefit to owning it. Merchandise is sitting in your store screaming buy me! It is up to the salesperson to hear that scream and give the customer a reason to heed it. Features and benefits are typically what most people think of as selling. This is why it is so important to earn a customer's trust before launching into features and benefits. Otherwise, you'll have a much tougher time closing the sale. With properly executed stages though, the close is easy.

5. Closing With an Add-On

Finally comes the close. Will they choose to purchase the product? There are loads of books on how to close a sale. They all include two of the worst and most over-used ways.

1. In **the assumptive close** the salesman assumes the customer has agreed to the sale and asks, "If I can arrange delivery on Tuesday or Thursday, are you prepared to buy today?"

2. In the **reduction-to-the-ridiculous close** the salesperson asks the customer, "How much too much is this?" After the customer answers, he continues, "So what separates us from making this deal is about $50. Is that right? And this product is going to last at least five years, wouldn't you say? So that's really only $10 a year. And that means it's less than a $1 a month. And isn't your happiness worth $1 a month?" I hate that crap.

> Because the truth is nobody likes to be closed.

If you use techniques like those to get customers to purchase your product or service, they'll often change their minds when they get home!

But if you've consciously gone through the five parts to a sale, you don't have to use any technique to close. It will happen naturally.

The close of a sale also offers you the opportunity to add on. We assume we've closed the sale so we suggest another product that goes with it. Some people call this suggestive selling.

For example, if they purchased a hot coffee drink you could add on with a suggestion that paints a picture. "How about a toasted onion bagel with cream cheese to go with that?" That is a great add-on. Contrast that to most coffee shops, independent or chain, where all you hear is, "Anything else?"

Is there a difference? Absolutely. Is it hard to do? No. Who benefits? Ultimately the customer because they are getting something they may not have thought about or known that you had. The company benefits from the additional sale and the employee, having gotten the higher ticket, gets a bigger tip or commission.

If your customers are going out your door with only one item, you have a staff of order takers. Your profit is in that second item. It makes no difference how great the store looks and how well the merchandise is arranged, if your crew does not actively suggest the add-ons, you're missing the boat.

Add On—No Matter What Your Business

At Nunn-Bush Shoe Shop in Glendale, CA, I trained the salesmen to carry around shoe trees. Cedar shoe trees take the moisture out of shoes so they last longer. Customers needed to know this. When a customer bought a pair of shoe trees, the salesperson got a spiff and as a result, unit sales were always among the highest in the nation.

If you are a hardware store, customers need to get the flashlight *and* the batteries. If you are a coffee house, they need to get the espresso drink *and* the pastry. If you are the eyeglass store, they need to get the reading *as well as* the sunglasses. If you are the clothing store, they need to get the pants *and* the belt. Any business needs to add on to a sale; that's where the profit is.

Conclusion to the Five Parts of a Sale

It should be every employee's goal to make people feel at home when they shop because people buy where there is a relationship, where they have a friend. Yes it's true some people are born friendly, but without knowing the five parts to a sale, they can monopolize the conversation and cost you business.

Training all of your employees on the five parts of a sale ensures that every person walking through your door deals with a salesperson, not a cashier. Just following these five points will help you to develop great relationships and make multiple-item sales.

If you've trained them well, salespeople aren't behind the counter waiting; they are active, moving around all the time. When they are untrained you get stories like this one:

In January of 1999, Men's Wearhouse launched a massive ad campaign. The ads were very well done; they promised great service and ended with the founder saying, "You're gonna love the way you look, you have my word on it." After seeing that ad, David Rutkoski and his fiancé Tracy went in to purchase a tuxedo. They spent a pleasant half-hour finding the perfect tux. When David paid for it, he told the salesman he needed it by the thirteenth. The salesman said, "No problem, I'll call and let you know when the alterations are done." He added, "I want to be here when you try it on and make sure it fits just right." Then he told David that he would help him choose the shirt and the proper accessories at that time.

> You must remember you are in the people business and that means employees are your biggest asset. Hire the best people, train them to be even better, and manage and reward them like family. Your store operation will be a place where people sell items, rather than customers browse them and you will finally be able to turn your attention to how to creatively market your business.

Time passed and even though his salesman hadn't called, David and Tracy went in to pick up the tux on the thirteenth. David didn't see his salesman and had to interrupt two others who were engaged in a conversation just to find out that he was not in that day. David gave his claim ticket to one of the salespeople. He immediately handed it to an employee, and ignoring David, resumed his personal conversation.

While David waited, he looked at shirts. He tried some on and liked them. No one said a word to him, even though there were no other customers in the store. Even though Tracy picked out a couple of additional suits for him. No one said a word. As time passed they became increasingly agitated and were concerned that the tuxedo wasn't even ready. The *salesmen* continued their conversation. Finally, David and Tracy noticed the tux hanging at the counter. David quickly tried it on for fit and said to Tracy, "That's it, we're out of here." Then they went to another store and purchased two suits and all the things he'd been looking for. His salesman lost a thousand dollars in add-on business that day. The chain lost more than ten times that amount when that night while being installed as president of the local Jaycee's, David, wearing his tux, told the story of his experience at the Men's Wearhouse.

CHAPTER 6

Check for Vital Signs
EMPLOYEE HIRING

Employees Are Your Most Important Asset

I resigned from Howard & Phil's as the result of a simple question at an upper-level management meeting. The company president asked, "What is our company's most important asset?"

Thinking this was a no-brainer, I piped up, "Our employees."

"Wrong," he responded. Stunned, I watched the others stumble for answers. When no one could arrive at the answer he obviously wanted to hear, he said, "Our customers."

I challenged, "A company does not own its customers—they can do whatever they want. Without the smiling faces and sales skills of our crew, we'd be nothing." The president disagreed.

For nearly thirty years Howard & Phil's had been a successful family business, an equilateral triangle: employees, merchandise and customers. Their employees' skills and personalities *transformed* lookers into buyers. Because of their *salespeople*, the chain was able to sell a variety of goods and expand. Because they had a *variety* of goods, it was able to satisfy a variety of customers.

But now the chain was faltering because the owners had implemented stringent requirements on managers. They had diminished bonuses, increased workloads and ended manager input. Their management handbook had tripled in rules and fines. The employees had become demoralized and disillusioned. Turnover had increased at all levels and resulted in untrained people manning the floors.

This was just a great joke to one of the owners who laughed and said, "We go through people so quickly that when I call one of our stores, I don't ask for the manager by name, I just say, 'Let me speak to whoever's in charge.'"

With the foundation of the triangle broken, it didn't take long for the quality of merchandise to diminish and for customers to notice.

This is where I began to understand a business owner's hubris that allows them to think customers will always be there, that owners can do whatever they want and continue to be rewarded.

I was right about employees being the most important asset of a company. Howard & Phil's lost their best managers and salespeople and ended up out of business a few years later.

If you don't want to end up like them, adjust your thinking to acknowledge that employees are your biggest asset. You need to be as picky about hiring your sales force as you are in selecting a fine jewel. That care begins with your hiring process.

HIRING

Listening, Above All Else, Is Required

A family shared a vacation cottage for the night. The mother asked at breakfast, "How did you sleep?"

The two boys answered, "Our room was hot. We were tossing and turning all night."

The mother replied, "I know what you mean. I had to get up and put a blanket on."

While this is amusing, it was a great example of people who genuinely thought they were communicating only to end up with a *Huh?* instead of understanding. People don't listen equally. Sometimes it's a matter of focus.

In sales, you only want people who can focus, comprehend and respond to what the customer is saying in front of the public. There is nothing worse than walking in to a specialty retailer, restaurant or coffee house and meeting an employee who doesn't listen. Behind a counter at a deli restaurant, I came face-to-face with such a person. When she asked what I wanted, I said "A six-inch chicken sub on white with green peppers." She put on her gloves and got ready to make the sandwich and asked, "Was that white or wheat?"

"White."

"And what did you want?"

"A chicken sub with green peppers."

"Was that a six- or twelve-inch?"

"Six-inch."

"What did you want on it?"

"Green peppers."

"Did you want cheese?"

"No, just the peppers."

"You don't want me to warm it up first?"

"Yes, I want it warm."

"Well you said something about it being cold."

"What are you talking about? I never mentioned anything about cold." As I looked down, she was preparing a twelve-inch sub. "Uh, that's supposed to be a six-inch."

"Oh, I really can't do two things at once."

"Then you are in the wrong business," I said.

How was this allowed to happen? Who hired her? This type of frustrating counter help will cost you business. Training probably wouldn't help, as she couldn't make connections between what she was doing and saying. As awful as it may sound, we have to admit some people are drowning in a sea of words they can't comprehend. They don't belong on the sales floor. They are so distracted by their working environment that they are doing well if they can focus on just one thing at a time.

In hiring, you have a choice. You can hire one person to work only the register and another person to do just the sandwich making, or you can pay more and have one person who can do more than one thing and make customers feel appreciated.

At the Interview—Make Them Sell Themselves

The first thing I do when I begin an interview is ask the applicant how they pronounce their name and what they prefer to be called. I then read their phone number out loud just to make sure it's right. I then ask them the first important question, "Why did you apply with us?" I want to hear a response that says why they *specifically* want to work *here*. I want to know they love the clothes *we* sell, or they really like *our* store atmosphere or *our* windows caught their attention. I accept all answers except *I need a job*; pity is not a reason to hire someone.

I then ask them to describe a usual day at the place they are currently working, including their responsibilities. This usually breaks the ice and I get a general feel about them. At this point they have made the same first impression on me as they would on a customer. If it is a negative one, I find a way to end the interview. If their response is positive, we continue and I ask two important questions:

- *Can you describe a specific problem with a customer and how you handled it?* I ask this for three reasons: one, to see if they are listening, two, to see if they are honest and three, to see if they have personal responsibility. I want them to describe a specific incident, one where they dealt with a *specific* problem. Sometimes, applicants lie and say they never had a problem situation with a customer. A person who answers that they never had a problem is not being honest with themselves or me; they are trying to appear perfect. I don't hire them because I don't believe them.

Then there is the applicant who just drones on about how to handle a customer problem in general. They only heard part of the question and have missed my emphasis on specific details. This person offers general excuses but doesn't handle customer complaints individually. Provided I like their general attempt, I will ask them again to describe a specific time. If they don't do it again, we're done.

• *Can you give me a specific time you had a problem with another employee and tell me how you handled it?* I won't hire a person who tells me they told their manager and he took care of it or one that complained but did nothing productive to resolve it. I want them to tell me how they approached the other employee, where the discussion took place and what the result was. I want to hear they were able to work it out with the employee out of range of customers and with no further incidents.

Next I get site specific. At a coffee house I give the following scenario. "You are at the register, fully trained and there is no one on duty to ask any questions. A guy walks in and orders an ice blended mocha. You ring it up and say, 'It comes to $3.50.' He says, 'You must be new. I know the owner Marty and I only pay $1.'" I stop and ask, "What do you do?" They must tell me they'd say, "Sorry, it is $3.50—there are no discounts." If they say they would give it to the guy for $1, I don't hire them. Some people would say it is good customer service. I believe it is thievery that they are willing to give away product based only on what someone said. If it is not thievery, it is at least a person who is naive enough to be swayed or conned. Either way, you lose. The only other acceptable answer would be to tell me that out of the goodness of their heart, they gave it to the guy for one dollar and paid for the rest out of their tips. In both cases $3.50 went into the cash register.

I then ask, "Can you give me five reasons I should hire you?" Lots of answers will suffice. I want to know they have enough self-esteem

to think they are worthy hires. They can respond with *I'm bubbly,*
I'm attractive, I'm dependable, I have a positive attitude, I'm never sick,
I get along well with others, I can do lots of things at one time, etc. I love
to hear they like our product and the store. I don't dwell on nuances
here; anything positive at all is good. Again, the quickest turn off is
the answer *because I need a job.* Pity is not a reason to hire anyone.
Let someone else hire them; otherwise, you'll be making excuses for
their performance to your staff, to your customers and to yourself. If
they cannot sell you on themselves with five reasons, how will they
ever sell a customer on your products?

If I liked the applicant's answers, I ask them to call me back at 4
pm the following day. This allows me time to check references (and
I always check). The person who calls me back at four o'clock on the
dot is usually going to be my best trainee. They start the next day
and begin a five-day training process. The ones who call much earlier are a bit too eager and those who are late, I don't hire.

CHAPTER 7

Make Them Hear You
EMPLOYEE TRAINING

W hen I was fifteen, I worked as a janitor. One day while the owner was on his honeymoon, his parents came in to manage things. I showed up in the afternoon and began cleaning. The owner's mom was a tough old bird right out of a Dickens novel. She called me over to the sink and said, "So you're the one! You call this clean?"

I shrugged my shoulders and said, "Yes."

"Are you afraid of getting your hands wet? Look at the ring around this sink! Clean it again!"

So I cleaned it again, but the stain didn't come out.

"You've got to use elbow grease!" With that she scoured the sink and the stain was gone. "I don't ever want to see something like that again!" She snarled and went away.

Did I hate her at that moment? You bet. Could she have trained me better? Absolutely. Was the sink ever dirty like that again? Not a chance. She yelled at me and I learned what her expectations were.

You need to adopt standards before any training can take place and every time you train, you must train to those standards. At the cleaners, the word *clean* meant something different to the mom than it did to her son. You need to be consistent with your expectations and let all your employees know what is expected of them.

Yes, good training is a lot of work. It's like the guy who said to me, "Training is too much money; what if they leave?" I countered, "What if you don't train them and they stay?"

Train with an Eye to the Exceptional Circumstance

I was at a Saturday workshop with forty or fifty hotel consultants on how to increase revenues. For twenty minutes the trainer, pretending to be an event organizer, had been calling local hotels. To each front desk agent, he became a different customer. It was obvious he was trying to trip them up with exceptional circumstances and requests. He asked about special features of the area, corporate room rates and even hosting wedding parties. We listened over the speakerphone to the ineffective responses by whoever had the misfortune to be at the front desk that morning. He enjoyed showing how his questions flummoxed them. Before picking up the phone again, he further insinuated that such poor employees would lead to lower sales. His point was that these hotels had hired dumb front desk agents.

I raised my hand, stood and said, "You know, I think this is really unfair and unprofessional. You are asking questions that these people obviously were not trained to answer. It is not their fault; no one wants to look like a jerk. All of those employees were doing their best even though they lacked the knowledge of how to assist you. Most were not rude or indifferent. **They were just not trained**." And with that, I sat down.

It was as if a bomb had gone off. The room was silent. The guy stopped calling hotels and immediately changed his tune. But I know he and the others won't forget my point that it was the managers' fault for the poor responses given—not the employees'.

The lesson for you is to give people all the knowledge you can when training them. Don't forget if they can't learn, let them go. But make the ones you keep prepared for anything, from how you want your place to look to how you want them to handle unusual inquiries. Otherwise they'll learn in front of your customers—the worst place of all.

Train as if They Wrote Your Paycheck—They Do

You wouldn't go away for several days and leave popular teenagers home alone without rules. You would give them boundaries, rules you'd expect them to follow and things you'd expect them to do. You'd leave them with a definite idea of what is accepted and what is not. Employees expect the same treatment.

If you do not train your employees, they have no context for their actions. If they say the wrong thing, your customers may get bad information, diminishing their chances of buying from you. Even if only one employee out of your whole crew gives bad service, you end up with all of your customers' experiences being at risk. You must give structure so every customer gets the same message. Scripts do this.

A Script Ensures Quality

In the previous hotel example, a well-devised script would have ensured that the front desk agents wouldn't be rattled by the questions. Once they realized that the customer needed to be directed to the Group Sales Manager who didn't work weekends, they should have been able to follow a scripted procedure laid out by the manager. They would have answered, "I'm sorry but the Group Sales Manager isn't in on Saturdays. I can take down all your information and give it to Ms. X tomorrow. May I get your name, address and phone number with your area code, your dates of arrival and departure, the number of rooms you need and any special requests?" The front desk agent would then read the information back to the customer. Once verified they'd say, "If you don't hear from her by noon, please feel free to call her on our 800 number which is xxx-xxxx. Thank you for calling." Click and done.

A script would have put them in charge of the situation. They would have gathered all the information so the Group Sales Manager could successfully return the call Monday morning. If the trainer had called such a hotel, he would have found an employee who had the tools to handle the situation and not appear stupid.

A few years ago, Barbara Streisand made a big comeback with a set of very high priced concerts. She got multiple standing ovations throughout her tour. Reviewers said she was relaxed, funny, sincere and quite entertaining. A few weeks later, the news came out that her performance was all scripted. Some critics had a field day with this. They said scripting made it artificial, canned and plastic. I disagree. I say if the music was uniformly emotional and well rehearsed, the speeches convincing and poignant, the jokes truly funny and the audience response to it all amazing, then the scripting worked.

When a script is consistently well-presented, it forms the framework of interactions between people whether they are guests, customers or actors. When done well, it sounds quite natural. Whether in New York or Seattle, by using a script, Streisand gave her audiences the experience they wanted. A script will do the same for your customers. They will get consistently high quality service without room for error.

Think of your last airplane experience. The stewards and stewardesses all had a script on how to ensure passenger safety. Why? Because if they didn't, people could get hurt and even die. It is no different in your business.

Write Your Own Script

A script walks an untrained person through a sale and allows a trained person to almost go into autopilot knowing how the process works. It highlights the features and benefits of a product before a customer asks. This keeps both the salesperson and the customer focused. Customers want to be led. They don't want to make a decision about something they know nothing about. Customers want to be helped and guided, especially if the product is unfamiliar and there are many choices.

There's not a lot of room for error during a scripted sale. You can script most parts of customer contact beginning with the greeting. A script for a coffeehouse could begin in many ways. *Welcome to Polly's; Welcome to the best place on earth; Welcome to coffee heaven; Welcome home.* Each of these evokes a particular feeling. You could combine them into a hybrid, *Welcome to Polly's, Long Beach's coffee heaven.* A good script doesn't give an employee the chance to use either of the worst greetings in the world, *Can I help you?* or *Who's next?* In addition, slang terms such as *How's it hangin'?* or *Whassup?* have no place in a your greeting. Most employees need to be reminded that they are to model more civil language than they use in their everyday lives.

As your employees (and you) get comfortable with your script, they are free to expand, personalize, etc. For example, twenty people in line don't want to hear the same parroted greeting. It says they are not customers and you are a robot.

Qualifying a customer as a friend is a skill that needs personalization and therefore cannot be scripted, but qualifying the person *as a customer*, can be. A qualifying script works like a funnel as it narrows the customer's focus by starting with the two biggest, most general categories, then focusing down to the specifics with succeeding questions. These questions have to systematically cut your store down into bite-size pieces. For a hardware store in a planned community, after I've greeted and qualified the customer as a friend, our scripted conversation begins:

"What's your project today?"

"I need paint."

"It's a great day for it. Interior or exterior?"

"Exterior."

"Do you live in the neighborhood?"

"Yes, in Bay View."

"That is such a nice area! We have a board over here with all of the approved exterior colors; you can just point to it. My favorite's Southwest Sienna; it blends in nicely with the canyon. All of our colors come in three qualities of paint and I can show you how they compare."

The right script funnels the customer down through a series of questions with an eye to looking ahead in the sale. A script helps you train employees with all sorts of knowledge that customers may not know. With no script, you don't have a funnel; you have a sieve with all sorts of questions leading to all sorts of results.

The same scenario with a friendly salesperson but without a script at the same hardware store:

"What's your project today?"

"I'm looking for paint."

"What color?"

"Sunshine yellow."

"That's always such a cheery color, isn't it? We have several versions of sunshine yellow. What are you going to paint?"

"My house."

"Great, how old is it?"

"Oh, about five years."

"Did you buy it new?"

"Yes, my wife and I picked it out when we came here from California."

"Oh, my cousin is from San Francisco. Have you ever been there?"

"No, we are from Los Angeles."

"Isn't the air quality great here?"

"Yeah, now about the paint. We're painting the outside."

"Stucco or wood?"

"Stucco."

"We have three that will do the job and this one is on sale for $6.99 a gallon and has a warranty."

"Great, I guess I need about four gallons."

"No, you'll need probably more like ten unless it is a very small house."

"OK, ten it is."

While the paint is being mixed, the manager happens to walk by. "Sunshine yellow in an exterior paint? You must not live around here."

"Actually, I live only a couple blocks away."

"Well then I hate to tell you, but you can't use that color. The homeowners' association does not approve it and you'll be fined if you do. Over here are your choices."

Because he had no script, the friendly salesperson asked all sorts of questions that led nowhere. If the manager hadn't shown up, the customer would have walked away with the wrong product, would have painted his house and been subsequently fined.

For coffeehouses, I created scripts for what to do when someone doesn't know what they want to drink. After qualifying them as a friend, the script moves on to:

"What can I make for you today?"

"I don't know."

"Do you think you would like something hot or cold?" This immediately reduces our choices in half.

"I guess something hot."

"Have you tried cappuccinos or lattes?"

"Yeah, I've tried them before."

"Did you like them?"

"Yeah."

"Maybe you'd like something sweeter?"

"What have you got?"

"One of my favorites is the Vanilla Latte. It's got the punch of an espresso but a with a creamy vanilla taste—it's one of our most popular. (It would be up to the employee to have one that they truly liked and was a best seller).

"Does that sound good?"

"Yeah, that sounds great!"

While you cannot possibly cover all the variations during the second part of a sale, a good script serves to limit pregnant pauses and contains the following elements:

- It cuts down the customer's choices. In these instances, the choice of paint color or hot or cold coffee began the funneling process. A furniture store script might separate indoor from outdoor furniture. A travel agent's script might separate business from vacation travel.

- A script shows knowledge of customer preferences and demands. No matter what the category, you must know your best selling items. With the coffee house the employee suggested the number one seller. In a travel agency it might be a certain vacation hotspot. In a furniture store, it might be a new styling trend.

- It builds in a place for the employee to genuinely say, *My favorite is*. In the sales process, people generally want to be led towards a decision. We are not there to make the decision for them, but having a personal favorite will let you start with something you feel good about. Remember, selling is nothing more than a transference of feeling. Because I feel good about something, so will you. That's why I suggest every coffee house barrista find a favorite drink within the most popular categories. I don't want someone recommending something most people wouldn't order.

- It includes opportunities to insert complimentary words about the customer's preferences or previous choices, comments based on either what the customer is choosing or has chosen in the past. Words like *great, nice* and *excellent* are what separates salespeople from order-taking robots—they are complimentary. The paint salesperson complimented the customer on their neighborhood, their choice of paint color and day to paint. Those compliments enhanced rapport between the customer and the salesperson.

Scripts can also present information that customers may not ask about your product but that they need to hear in a specific order.

At Howard & Phil's all my employees had to tell boot customers that new boots, when first put on, will slip in the heel and feel snug in the front. Consider the following two scenarios:

Without a script, Ms. Customer asks, "Do you have this boot in a 7?"

"Yes, here you go."

Ms. Customer pulls on the boot and says, "Hey these slip in the heel."

"Oh yeah, they're supposed to do that."

"But the front feels tight."

"Oh yeah, new boots do that."

"How long will it do that?"

"Until they break in."

"Uh huh." She takes off the boot and says she'll look around. Next thing you know, she's gone.

With a script, you greet Ms. Customer when she comes in, qualifying her as a customer and a friend, then she asks, "Do you have this in a 7?"

While you are waiting for her to remove her shoes, you say, "Have you worn boots before?"

She answers, "No."

"When boots are new they will slip in the heel and the foot will feel a bit snug. The sole will relax as you break them in which takes about a week of wearing them."

She tries on the boot and says, "Yeah these *do* seem to be loose in the heel."

"Remember, I told you that?" you say with a smile, careful not to smirk.

"Let me walk around in them."

"How do they feel?"

"They are a still bit snug up front."

"That'll go away in about a week."

She comes back, sits down and buys them.

In the first scenario, the salesperson was on the defensive, reacting to the customer. He was correct in what he said, but because the information was presented in response to the questions, it let the customer think he was just a bit dishonest in trying to make the sale.

The second scenario *with the script* puts the salesman in the place of knowledge and power. Because the negative qualities were presented beforehand, the customer knows what to expect and feels the salesperson can be relied on for further information.

This is a step up from various boot stores that tell the new boot buyer nothing. They leave them to come back and return the boots because they were sloppy in the heel. Trying to placate the disappointed customer, the store personnel tell the truth about the break-in period. By then though, the trust and relationship are gone.

If you have a strict return policy—that can get sticky around Christmas—a script to address it might be, "You can return anything you buy today for a complete refund with your receipt—except sale items. Without a receipt or on sale items, we can give you store credit." That's all any customer wants to hear. Contrast this to someone buying a sale item for Christmas:

"Is this blouse on sale?"

"Yes, it is 40 percent off."

"Can I get my money back if she doesn't like it?"

"No, there are no refunds on sale items."

Suddenly the customer feels trapped; there are no options and the sale is in jeopardy.

Sometimes you establish a script because you want to make sure customers understand the best features of your products and their benefits.

When I came to the Bay Shores Inn in Newport Beach, the owner, Bill Pratt, had a check-in speech he personally used any time he welcomed a guest.

"We have a breakfast room right over here," he said, walking the guest to the room as he talked. "We have fresh baked muffins, pastries, as well as both hot and cold cereals. The drink and ice machines are in the courtyard," he continued motioning out the door. "You can check out any of our 150 videos to watch in your room tonight. If you need help deciding on a restaurant, any of the guys at the front desk can help you. If you like seafood, the Crab Cooker is my favorite. Finally, there's someone here twenty-four hours a day so if you need anything, just ask. Enjoy your stay with us!"

What a great script! Bill said, "I used this because right from the start, I wanted to give the customers something back for their money instead of just handing them the key and sending them to a room. There was a lot I wanted them to know right away. They were giving me their money, and I was giving them more than a room. They could get that anywhere." I decided to make this the basis for a reservation script.

Since the Bay Shores Inn had room rates well over $100 per night, quoting the price first had led many people to hang up before they heard the inn's benefits. To thwart this, I developed a rather extensive script. Now when anybody calls for reservations, the conversation goes like this:

"This is Ted, how can I help you?"

"How much is a room?"

"For what day of arrival?"

"For Friday."

"For how many nights?"

"Just one."

"For how many people?"

"Two, me and my wife."

"How many beds?"

"Just one."

"Great, have you stayed with us before?" If they say, "No," the front desk agent continues.

"While I check availability, may I tell you a bit about us?" Callers always say *yes*. Then Ted begins the second part of the script. "We're about a hundred paces between the bay and ocean beaches. We are located just three blocks from the Newport Pier. All twenty-five of our non-smoking, air-conditioned rooms come with a breakfast buffet with fresh bagels, muffins, pastries, fruit and both hot and cold cereals. You can actually eat breakfast here. We have everything for a great day at the beach including towels, umbrellas and even boogie boards, so you don't have to pack them. All our rooms have a VCR, and you can check out any of our 150 videos for free." Ted by now has checked the computer and knows if he has a room or not. If he has a room available, he tells them the various room options (bay view, standard, suites, etc.) for that day and gives them the rate for each.

Notice the script emphasized the value of the Inn before price ever came up. Also, it shared the features and benefits returning guests have told us they appreciated.

If the person had said, "Yes," they *had* stayed with us before, the script is shorter but reminds the customer of the values the Inn offers. "Great, so you know about the free breakfast buffet, the beach equipment and the videos, right?" Everyone must get the same information.

Once all of the reservation details are finished, there is a final script that says, "We have a forty-eight hour cancellation policy. If you do have to cancel, please write down your cancellation number at that time." This prevents people from saying they didn't know our policy or that they called yesterday to cancel or that we didn't give them a number. We then continue, "Check in is at three; check out is at eleven." We don't want them showing up at noon saying the front desk agent said they could. "All the rooms are non-smoking. There is a $150 charge if anyone smokes inside the rooms." We mean business! "Do you know how to get here?" If they don't, the script offers detailed instructions including land-marks on how to get to the Inn. "Your reservation is for (repeating the day of arrival, number of days, number of guests, number of beds at a rate of). This ensures we have the correct information and that the rates have been agreed to. "Have I answered all of your questions?" This gives them the space to make sure we covered everything that is important to the guest.

By asking if they have any questions, you make customers feel comfortable enough to ask anything. In the past we have been asked if we have a free shuttle, baby-sitting service, florist, even if there is a liquor store nearby. We then say, "Here's your confirmation num-ber. We look forward to seeing you (their name inserted here) next week (or month)."

By developing a relationship at the front desk, guests immediate-ly felt special. The experience was different from any of the hotels in Newport Beach. Even though the Bay Shores Inn is a small hotel with no concierge, no restaurant or pool, revenues doubled in the past five years. The scripts used at the Bay Shores concentrated on what they had to offer that the other guys didn't. That is the basis of a great script.

All employees who might ever answer the phone or come in cus-tomer contact must memorize all of the scripts within the first day.

Train with a Checklist to Ensure Standards

Good training emphasizes building customer relationships and people skills. A checklist guarantees this by giving a concise day-by-day training process with specific points that every employee must master before they are able to work on their own. Each day the new hire learns something about sales, product knowledge and store procedures. Each day begins with a review of the previous day's training.

Training without a checklist goes something like this. "Hi, I'm supposed to train you today on how to make coffee. It's really easy. I'm sure you do it a lot at home. Just watch me for a while and then I'll give you a chance to try." Time passes. "Any questions? I mean it's really simple. Take coffee, grind it and put in a filter, then press the button and brew. Voila! Now you try." Of course, knowing *how* to measure and grind the beans, *when* to brew and *what* to do if the brewer doesn't work and other details are never mentioned. To a casual observer, the employee was trained. Whoa be it when, on a busy Saturday morning, the brewer overflows and coffee gushes to the floor! Because there were holes in their knowledge that you missed when you could have trained them with a checklist, the employees invariably learn but many times in front of a customer.

Without a checklist, it's amazing what unsupervised trainers might impart. Mike Sheldrake, owner of Polly's Gourmet Coffee, related the following story. It was Christmastime when a longtime employee came up to him and asked, "Since I didn't take my free pounds of coffee all year, can I just get my ten free pounds today?"

"What do you mean?"

"Well, the guy who trained me told me that every month every employee gets to take home a free pound of whatever coffee they want, and I haven't done it like everyone else. Can I?"

Mike was so shocked all he could say was *NO*. He knew he had no such policy. With a dozen or so employees, he wondered how much revenue he'd already lost. The practice stopped immediately.

Create a Five-Day Training Checklist

Begin by writing down everything you think someone should know about your business under these five categories: Human

Relations, Policies, Procedures, Product Knowledge, and Sales. Your list of specific points is meant to jog the trainer's memory, lead them to train exact procedures, relate stories and share examples of what happens when you follow procedures well. After you have all of your categories written, decide if you've missed anything major or if any are petty. Add and delete accordingly.

Now go back through and put them in order. See what logically should flow from one to the other within those categories. For example, you don't want to tell a trainee to price pants until they know where the pants are in your store, where the price sheets are kept or where the price gun is located.

Once you have a flow within the five categories, prioritize them into an order that builds from the basics to the most advanced. You want to train how to clock-in before you train how to do vendor returns.

You may not get it all perfect the first time you train someone with your new checklist. If you find something that doesn't fit logically or was missed, *change your checklist immediately* so the next time you won't make that mistake again. Once developed, stick to making sure every single category and specific point is covered and checked off.

For most clients, Day One includes a tour of the facility, basic store policies, basic training on the register, introductions and a background and history of the store. After the basics are covered, the trainee gets their first script, the exact words they will use as they move through the five parts to a sale. They need to have it memorized by the following day. On the next page is the one I created for the Bay Shores Inn.

Check off and collect as complete:

___ Application	__ Reference/ Previous Job Check	___ CA EDD Form
___ W-4	__ CA Disability Insurance	___ Employee Folder
___ I-9	__ Worker's Comp	___ Employee History
___ Sexual Harassment Is Forbidden		___ Job Description

Check off after trainer has discussed with employee:

___ Emergencies: Fire, Earthquake, Robbery, Water Heater, Plumbing, Elevator

___ No Show/Tardiness/Probation/Warnings/Schedules

___ Location of supplies for front desk, maids, computers, breakfast room

___ Smoking and Drug Policy

___ Dress Code and Dismissal policy

___ Injury on the Job

___ Employee Parking, Time Cards, Breaks, Tour of Hotel

Before continuing to Day Two, employee must complete this section:

___ I have viewed all the training tapes (circle as viewed) 1 2 3 4 5 6 7

___ I am familiar with and understand: guest service, the 5 parts to a sale, negotiating rates, telephone policy, how to complete Housekeeping Report, LEA and Check-out report, and set up the breakfast room.

___ I know how to check someone in and out, how to complete reservations, credit card transactions, and how to sign out loan equipment.

___ I know what the uniform standards are, how to operate the computer and the reservation script.

"I have read and checked off the above as requested. If I have any questions regarding the above, they have been answered. By signing below, I understand the position for which I was hired is demanding and requires my absolute concentration, excellent interpersonal skills and superior communication abilities. I also agree that I am 100% trustworthy and a go-getter. I have a positive attitude and understand many of the assignments are broad-based and require common sense judgments on a regular basis."

_____

Employee Signature   Date

_____

Trainer Signature   Date

Day Two training for a coffee shop begins with a review of the major growing areas and a sampling of the five taste profiles from each region. On Day Three, you could show how the same coffee, made four or five different ways, tastes differently. In addition, you could quiz them on the five regional taste differences from the previous day. On Day Four, training would focus on the premium estate grown coffees like La Minita Terrazu and the stories of how each family controls all aspects of coffee production from the bean to the cup. On Day Five, you'd have the trainee teach you about all the coffees covered and then give them a final quiz.

DAY TWO	DAY THREE	DAY FOUR	DAY FIVE
__ Areas	__ Brewing	__ Estates	__ Teach
__ Samples	__ Review	__ Families	__ Quiz

Day Two training for a paint store begins with the basic differences between types of paints, varnishes and stains. Day Three could be your private label paint vs. the competitors' and how yours stands up better. Day Four could be about effects you can get with various colors, brushes and sponges to achieve a variety of effects. On Day Five, you'd have them try painting something with your best seller and role-play helping someone get setup to paint their house.

DAY TWO	DAY THREE	DAY FOUR	DAY FIVE
__ Paints	__ Our Brand	__ Effects	__ Use
__ Varnishes	__ Competition	__ Colors	__ Role-play

In a women's clothing store, Day Two would begin with the different pant lines you carry and whether or not they have matching tops. On Day Three, you cover all your jeans, the various fits, contrasting features and benefits of each with attention to price points. Remember, you want to make sure they aren't comparing apples to apples and telling customers that this jean is more expensive than that one unless they know *why*. Day Four could show how to take care of denim and the common causes of returns, shrinkage, etc.

Day Five could be watching training videos from various manufac-turers followed by a quiz.

DAY TWO	DAY THREE	DAY FOUR	DAY FIVE
__ Pants	__ Jeans	__ Denim	__ Videos
__ Tops	__ Prices	__ Extras	__ Quiz

On Day Two at a shoe store, my checklist continued to get more detailed and required every salesman to learn how to use a Brannock device to measure feet. After they could demonstrate consistently that they could read the device, they were taught to measure each and every customer's foot. It didn't matter if the customer knew he took an 8 D, we measured them. Why? Because left and right feet often vary by up to one size. If a guy had very narrow or wide feet, or if his instep was too high or low, it would automatically limit the choices the salesman had to work with. Having understood why we measured everyone, the salesperson was trained to match up the cus-tomer's foot before going to the stockroom. That way, if the cus-tomer had limited options, the trainee could collect all of his choic-es at once, saving the customer time and maximizing the sales opportunities. This step also kept trainees from going into features and benefits on the sales floor about why a particular product was so well made or why it would fit a customer's foot, only to go to the stockroom and find there was no shoe in the customer's size.

Day Three required the new hire to try on every shoe we had in their size so they knew how each one fit. He learned which shoes fit sloppy, which were tight, which felt better than others. This way if a customer found a shoe that fit particularly well, the salesman didn't waste their time trying to find others that *might* fit; he *knew* and could present additional pairs easily and with certainty. In addition, all the salespeople had to pay attention from one sale to the next to build their product knowledge. This was particularly true for the saleswomen who couldn't try on the shoes and had to rely on what other salesmen and customers told them.

Day Four's checklist continued with how to suggest and match up available stock, based on customer comments. This knowledge allowed the salesperson to leave the door open to several shoe choices before going to the stockroom, should one particular shoe style be out of stock. On Day Four, the salesperson would learn to bring out four boxes of shoes; the requested pair, a pair in the same color, but different style, the originally requested pair in another color and a casual. After the customer decided on the original pair, he would invariably ask the salesperson, "What's in those boxes?" This would allow the salesperson to say, "I found a few others in the back. Do you mind if I show you a few more in your size?" The customer would, ninety-nine out of one hundred times, answer yes. They'd often buy two or three pairs of shoes where many shoe stores would have sold just one.

On Day Five, my shoe salespeople learned that as a shoe gets longer, the width goes down one letter; a 7 1/2 E is the same width as an 8 D. Maybe you don't have a 9 D, but if you have an 8 1/2 E, it just might fit. If it doesn't, at least the salesperson was proactive instead of saying, "No, we don't have that one in your size" resulting in the customer leaving with no options. This sometimes took more than one day to train but was crucial in making additional sales. Notice that such technical information was reserved for the final day after the trainee had a good background in the stockroom and in how to fit a shoe properly.

Day Five finished with the trainee role-playing with me as a difficult to fit customer.

DAY TWO	DAY THREE	DAY FOUR	DAY FIVE
__ Brannock	__ Try on	__ Door Open	__ Widths
__ Stockroom	__ Match up	__ Four pair rule	__ Role-play

How to Train with Your Checklist

Your trainer should be a person with lots of energy and patience because let's face it, training involves a lot of repetitive work. But often store owners don't *want* to train every employee every time, so they put the new hire with *someone* more experienced and tell them to *train* the new hire. So *what* do they train? How to answer the phone, count the drawer, find the bathroom and identify the jerks in the store. Meanwhile mastering sales techniques, learning the regulars' names and knowing the finer points of making a relationship are all out the window. You are left with a haphazard program of dregs training dregs.

If you will not be training everyone yourself, train your best employee to teach the new hires. They need to realize even with a checklist, there is a procedure to training that must be followed. For instance, since the mind can only concentrate for about twenty minutes at a time, at that point trainers need to put down the checklist and have their trainee do something menial; have them take out the trash, sweep the floor or complete paperwork, etc. before proceeding to the next bite-size point on the list.

The important thing to learn from all of these examples is to break down into manageable bite-sized pieces all of the information you are carrying around in your head. Start with things that are most critical or basic to your business. If you are a blind store, have them learn how to measure a window from day one and repeat each day. If you are a coffee house, have them learn how to keep the place spotless. Make sure that all information can be easily learned and tested. If you start out to teach them everything you know without a checklist, you'll be spinning your wheels.

As a trainer you need to prepare a training time when you can be free of interruptions and obligations for at least twenty minutes. You need to instruct the trainee before beginning, that if you must leave for any reason, they should again keep themselves busy by sweeping the floor, taking out the trash or wiping off the counters. Tell them that under no circumstances should they just stand at the counter with their arms folded, waiting. You also need to inform them about what to tell a customer if they are asked a question. New hires hate being put in the position of having to say, "I don't know. I'm new here," as much as customers hate hearing it.

At the beginning of the session, tell trainees what they are going to learn and how they will be expected to demonstrate it by the end of the day. Ways of demonstrating can include role-playing, an oral quiz or even a written test. Let them know if they don't master it, you will work with them on it again tomorrow. If they get it right, you continue with their training, which puts them closer to earning tips, bonuses or commissions. If the trainee doesn't meet your expectations, you must decide hiring them was a mistake and part company.

If you are about to train them on something you think they already know, tell them why you are showing them this. For example, while coffee houses hire lots of people with previous training, each new hire needs to know how you want them to pull a shot of espresso in *your* store, steam the milk for *your* drinks and how hot *your* drinks are to be served. Everything needs to be understood as exclusive to your store.

Show the trainee one specific aspect of the job they'll be doing. Tell them to watch while you make an iced drink just like you usually do. Next offer only a cursory explanation to give the trainee a quick overview of what they will be learning. This is not the time for the trainee to ask questions. Then go back over it slowly, demonstrating exactly *how* and telling *why* something was done. At key points *ask* the trainee if they understand what you are doing. Discuss the exact way you want things done: drink consistency, safe food handling and occupational hazards. Tell them they are free to ask questions at any time during this learning stage.

Next, have them repeat the process you just taught them while you watch. Let them know it is still all right to ask questions any time they feel unsure. Don't let them deviate at all from your technique; keep it to the exact standards you've set. Practice until they get it right at speed, always more than once. Just like scripts, consistency is what this is all about.

Now have them explain to you in their own words the process that they were taught. This enables you to find out if you missed something important in the training. It will be crystal clear as long as you don't coddle them. Don't lead them or let them ask questions during awkward moments of silence.

Finally, have them physically repeat the process one more time. If they do it correctly, you sign off on the checklist that this part of their training has been accomplished, and you are ready to move on to the next point on the list.

This training works for any how-to aspect of a job. From how to ring the register to how to empty the trash. From how to cut a piece of glass to how to mix paint. From how to receive deliveries to how to ship special orders.

When their training is over, I have them sign their Day One checklist which includes, "I have been trained on how to do my job. If I have any questions, they have been answered. I certify I am a 100 percent go-getter and am prepared to do the job for which I was hired." This again lets them know you have standards. Should you get in a place where someone needs a written warning, you can refer back to the training checklist and the job description to affirm the employee was properly trained.

Open the Dressing Room Door to Higher Sales

On Day Four in my western wear training, the checklist taught employees to stay with customers when they went to the dressing room. I'd ask the trainee, "How many times have you gone into a store, picked up what you thought was your size and headed to the dressing room, only to discover the item didn't fit? And how many times was a salesperson there to help you? In this day and age, I would venture to say never. Yet it was something smaller stores used to pride themselves on. The number one way to lose customers is to be indifferent. We always want to be close by for them."

I would continue, "When a guy or a gal picks up a few things to try on, open the door for them and hang the clothes in the dressing room. Tell them, 'I'll be right outside if you need something.'"

"While they are in there, grab another garment. When they come out to look in the mirror say, 'I think this would go great with that.' People who thought they wouldn't like the garment on the rack are willing to give it a chance in the dressing room; provided you built up their trust during the first two stages of the sale. If you have developed rapport but get rebuffed and you think it really would look good on them, smile and say, 'Just try it on.'"

"This technique works particularly well on guys. They'll bring in a pair of jeans and try them on. If the jeans don't fit, they'll be out of there quick. Always stay by the dressing room and ask them questions before they have a chance to leave. It is up to you to run back and forth to find the perfect fit."

"Once you find it, you can show the customer the range of colors and fabrics we have in that same fit. Since guys don't like to shop, they often end up buying three or four pairs along with some shirts to go with them. You need to add on to every sale if you want to make bonus money."

Once a person is properly trained, they can contribute to your sales team. How you successfully manage that team of individuals is a test of your people skills and ultimately, how you avoid the icebergs.

CHAPTER 8

Building Your Team
SALES MANAGEMENT

S uccessfully managing your crew is not easy because people work in different ways. Understanding the different types of salespeople will help you build a sales team. There are always a couple of very good salespeople whose numbers are regularly at the top and who are competitively trying to outdo each other. Then there is the one salesperson who quietly does his own thing and gets big sales. There is the new kid who knows nothing but has all the enthusiasm in the world and gets big sales. There is the renegade who will do anything she or he can to be number one, even if it includes stealing other people's sales. And there is the trainee who knows nothing and you wish you hadn't hired in the first place. Bringing all of these diverse personalities and skill levels together into a cohesive team *can* happen, but it takes planning.

Your two competitive guys have to crow about their achievements. You need to give them the tools to do this. Their motivations become how you answer their question, "What's in it for me?" Contests, awards, plaques, bonuses and atta-boys are what keep these types around. They think all the attention they get is deserved, and sometimes they have to be taught how to say thanks.

The quiet salesperson is more typically in the *I am here to help the customer* mode than the others. She or he genuinely wants to help customers. While they don't outwardly demand attention, they need it just as much and will always thank you for it.

The new kid is excited just to come to work at your store. They've usually had no formal training in sales. *Beginner's luck* is frequently seen because new hires don't have all the baggage of rejection coloring the way they listen to a customer. But their energy and enthusiasm often leads them to overstate or understate certain features and bene-fits of your product. Be there for them with an ear to add or correct things, but don't squash their energy. While this enthusiasm is fun to have on the floor, it usually passes within six weeks. Just be ready to see if they can become more professional like the two top salespeople.

The renegade is the *What's in it for me?* taken to the max. Although they are often the funniest and most charming, they are selfish and will do anything to get their way. They add things in for free to make a sale and ring their returns on other employee's num-bers. Instead of working with the team, they do nothing but wait for customers to enter. If a window opens in the sale where they can exaggerate or tell the customer what they want to hear, they'll do it.

Left uncontrolled, the renegade will misrepresent your products. Due to their overstatements and lies, you have to deal with angry return customers. While an element of the renegade can be in all of your crew, it can be deadly if allowed to run rampant. If everyone is only interested in their *up*, a term used by commissioned sales peo-ple to make sure everyone has an equal shot at the customers, you get employees arguing on your sales floor about whose sale it was and who got credit if someone came back. Be consistent. Develop a policy and stick with it. My own policy was that once a customer left, the salesperson lost rights to the sale, unless the customer came back and asked for them by name. This encouraged salespeople to take more time trying to close the sale. What I didn't want was a group of employees running around giving out business cards with their names scrawled on them asking the customer to come back and ask for them—leave that behavior to the car dealers.

A renegade's behavior usually cannot be corrected without getting rid of the renegade. However, if you keep them on a short enough leash, they can be your best asset.

Personally I liked the renegades. One of my most memorable was Lou. He would be your best friend to your face, yet say some of the rudest things behind your back. Like most renegades, Lou was a scheming little boy. I was constantly amazed at some of the things that came out of his mouth. I called them my *Oh my God!* moments.

One day a woman asked how much a particular vest was. Because of the way she was dressed, Lou told her, "More than you can afford." My mouth dropped open. She came right back with, "How do you know how much I can afford?" Lou got out of it by saying, "With all those bags, how could you have money any left?" He amazingly made the sale because he was capable of a fast, bright comeback. Renegades are good at that. But the danger these types thrive on can be nerve racking.

Finally, if you have a trainee who you wished you hadn't hired, don't let them linger. Just get rid of them. You'll feel better and they won't frustrate the rest of the crew or your customers.

Hold Weekly Staff Meetings

Have a meeting with your crew one morning a week, an hour before your store opens. Use this time to go over sales for the month, policies and procedures, product knowledge, contests and prizes, inspirational sales stories and role-playing. This keeps your crew focused on what you expect. To grow their own leadership style, senior employees who have been with you a year or more and who have heard most of your stuff should share responsibility for running these meetings.

Meeting Tips
- Weekly
- Be Prepared
- Role-Play
- Have Fun
- Summarize

Towards the last ten minutes of one meeting a month, devise a contest that pits two groups of employees against each other. When I was at Howard & Phil's, I often had them see which team could build the biggest add-on sale. They invented a sales scenario then ran around the store selecting items that this fictional customer would buy. At the end of five minutes both teams would have a pile of clothes, boots and accessories and an explanation of why they chose what they did. Performing this exercise improved their sales skills; they had fun doing it and ultimately they thought about add-ons more often.

I'd wrap up each meeting by going around the room asking each person, "What did you learn new today?" or, "What did we talk about today?" That way I was sure everyone was actively listening.

Thirty Is the Best You Can Expect—Don't Settle

The new employee is going to be at their best during your thirty-day probationary period. This is where you must show the new hire that you inspect what you expect. If you start out as their friend, you're sunk. Your management style is on trial here, and they will find out what is acceptable by how consistent you are at enforcing your standards. So if your new hire is late on day two, realize she is testing you. Make clear to her what your tardy policy is, and that if it happens again, she'll be gone. If she breaks the policy twenty days later, fire her; she won't magically get better. And remember, your other employees are watching you.

If they snap at a customer, they are gone immediately. If you find them constantly talking to other employees, distracting them from their work, let them go. If you tolerate any of it during the first thirty days, I guarantee it will only get worse. One bad apple does indeed spoil the barrel.

I make the first month the toughest month. I always schedule a new hire's first shift for a busy day like Saturday. I want to see if they come in dragging after a busy night on the town. If they do, they should quickly learn they can't. If they do it again, we talk. "Don't you realize," I'd ask them, "that you can't stay out late the night before and be ready to work at 6 a.m.?" If they do it again, they are fired. If they call in sick instead, they are also fired. At the hotel I scheduled new maids on Sundays when we have all the checkouts. If they couldn't get all their rooms cleaned like the other maids, we'd talk. If they didn't speed up, they were gone. At a tire store the new hire should start on Monday when all the problems from the weekend need to be dealt with. If their people skills aren't great, they're gone.

The idea in all of these cases is to get them used to the highest stress first because then everything else will be a breeze.

Always Teach to Observe

One of the best ways to train is in an actual sales situation. I stand with a recent hire and we both observe a seasoned, successful salesperson. At the outset I'll ask the new hire what they noticed about the potential customer. Was there anything they were wearing, carrying or saying that would provide a **Window of Contact?** At South Coast Plaza I'd point out the clues: the name of the golf course on a man's shirt, a woman's fancy wedding ring or a Tiffany bag on an elaborate stroller.

By taking a quick inventory of what a potential customer is wearing or carrying, you can get an idea of their level of buying. The man wearing the Rolex watch and the man wearing the Timex are both equally deserving of every bit of a salesperson's time. However, the man who can afford the best watch probably can afford the best footwear. You can't help but make a judgment call if you are observant. Chances are less likely that a customer will spring for something far afield from their past choices. That means the person driving a Bentley who says they want something *cheap* won't be satisfied with a $100 boot when they regularly wear Ferragamos.

On the other hand, don't prejudge the customer who comes in with shabby clothes. Oftentimes these are the people who pay cash for the best products. You get their level of buying in the sales process when, noticing the price, they don't flinch.

Finally, good observation skills allow a salesperson to know when to close a sale. Whenever a customer is envisioning how they will use or take care of something means money in the bank. Buying signs include a customer asking how to take care of a garment or asking if they can get their name embroidered on an item. Train your new hires that when the best salespeople see and hear such buying signs, they know the sale is complete and close the sale by adding on. Have your new hires observe your best sales people from the time a customer walks in until they walk out, bags in hand.

Challenge Yourself to Show How to Do It Right

Ultimately, the success of your store depends on you. You must be able to lead by example. One of my most memorable sales happened at Howard & Phil's when I challenged myself to save a major sale. Everyone in the store was watching to see if what I taught really worked.

I had trained all of my salespeople to keep customer information cards on anyone who spent over $100 on a single purchase. These cards contained the customer's name and address, a record of their purchases, sizes, brand preferences and notations on any products they had considered buying. Using these cards, my crew sent out special handwritten invitations to our best customers the week before the Anniversary Sale.

That Saturday afternoon the store was busy. People were everywhere when I realized Lyle was stuck at the back of the store with one guy and a half dozen boots. I realized this sale could make or break our month so I challenged myself to accept responsibility for the sale in front of my salesmen. I walked up to a frustrated Lyle, faced the customer and began,

"What fits?"

"All of them except those two."

"Great, let's put these away," I said handing them to Lyle. You always want to find out what does and doesn't fit before you move on to the close of a sale. Otherwise the customer looks at all the trouble they've caused you and tends to back out. They've been overwhelmed with their choices. *What fit? What worked?* You get the idea.

"Do you like the colors?"

"Yes."

"Do they add to your wardrobe?"

"Yes."

"Did he mention that these had (I put in a few features and benefits of each of the boots)?"

"Yes." Always mention about three things you know you'll get a positive answer on before going on to the next question.

"Is there some reason you aren't taking these today?" Never give them help with these answers.

"Yes, the place down the street is having a big sale and I'm going to go back there and get them from that place."

"Really. Why is that?"

"They have these lizard boots for $100 less."

"I didn't know they carried this boot."

"Well, it's lizard."

"Yes, but it is not the same boot. Let me show you a similar one from that company," I said pulling a pair off the shelf. "You see how this one is pieced together? That's how come it's $100 less. Unfortunately, those pieces weaken the leather. When the skins get older, they tend to rip at those seams. Part of the reason the boots you've selected fit better is that they are one piece; these skins demand a premium. By the way, did they have your size?"

"No, but they said they could get them for me."

"And how long would that take?"

"They said a couple of weeks. But I can wait."

"So you think you'll get a better deal at the other place, even though it is not the same product and you'll have to wait?" I summed up the customer's objections in my own one sentence.

"Yes."

"I can understand you want the best value. I can understand you want to make the right decision. I understand you want to be taken care of. I can assure you, no one gets a better deal than you."

He elaborated that anyone could get what we were offering him, that there was nothing special about his deal.

"That's where you are wrong. Because we think you are such a great customer, we kept a card with your name and address so we could make sure you wouldn't miss this sale. We also knew what you liked and didn't like so we transferred in boots from three other stores in your size so you had this selection. My salesperson has spent the past hour making sure all of them fit properly. He also polished everything this morning so they would look their best—just for you." Which he had done. I continued, "If you get home and don't like something, we'll let you return it. The other guys won't. Is their sale price on a different boot going to make that big an impression on you? Well, whatever you feel is right. But I can tell you no one gets a better deal than you today." He stared at me silently. "The boots fit, the price is right, which of the five pair are you going to wear out of here?"

"Can you give me a pair of socks?" That was the buying sign. It meant I'd closed the sale; the rest was just details, and everyone could breathe easier.

"Nope, but it's good to get several pairs—and the trees to go with them. Which pair of boots do you want to wear home?"

And with that, we had a sale of several thousand dollars. Yes, I realize to some people that interaction will be seen as pushy. I look at it as helping the customer justify in his own mind what he want-ed and giving him permission to buy it.

Why did this work? I had a relationship with him previously, my salesperson had a relationship with him and I knew I could talk with him that way. I stood my ground and wouldn't let a competitor's lower prices get in my way. I knew what the personal connection was really worth—and it wasn't in the form of a discount or coupon. That customer enjoyed his purchase and came back several times over the years.

While it could have gone the other way and I could have lost the sale, if I hadn't challenged myself we definitely would have lost it.

No One Leaves without You Knowing Why

You need to be the eyes and ears of your store. You need to know everything that is coming in, going out, arriving at the back door, and leaving out the back door. That means you need to know your stock better than anyone. If a customer leaves without something, ask your salesperson what happened.

It was the last day of the month at Howard & Phil's when I saw one of my salespeople say good-bye to a Hispanic customer after having been with him for quite a while. I asked the salesman what happened. He said we didn't have the customer's size in the boot he wanted. I said it looked like he wanted lizard boots; he'd been trying them on for nearly an hour. The salesperson agreed but said we didn't have a 9 in the brown lizard. I asked, "The El Dorado 9254?" He said, "Yes." "I know we have it here somewhere," I said. "You need to go back and look in the stockroom; I'm sure you'll find it. Then you need to go into the mall and find him." The salesman looked at me like I was nuts and said with a sarcastic smile, "Yeah, right." The challenge was on.

I went in the back and, low and behold, there was the pair of $400 boots in a differ-

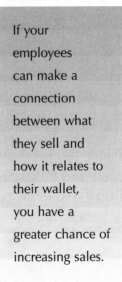

If your employees can make a connection between what they sell and how it relates to their wallet, you have a greater chance of increasing sales.

ent colored box but it was clearly labeled. I grabbed them. I went out on the sales floor. "See," I said. Then, holding one boot, I hurried out into the mall searching for the man and his family. (Since the customer had been in the store for nearly an hour, this made spotting him easier than it might sound.) I found him, but since I didn't speak Spanish, I had to motion and pantomime. The customer caught on and he and his family followed me up to the second level and halfway down another wing of the mall to the store. He purchased the boots and several outfits. I gave the salesperson credit for the sale and told him two things:

1. Double-check your stock. If you don't find something, ask someone to check around for you before the customer leaves, especially if it is expensive.

2. Never doubt me on sales procedures or stock again or you'll be gone.

Because I was willing to take ownership of the sale, we made our sales goal for the month and my employees received commission. You need to always be the best in your store. You need to be ready to use every sale as an opportunity to teach.

Discounting Doesn't Build Relationships

Wal-Mart can charge incredibly low prices because they get discounts from the manufacturers that you don't. When you discount, you make no profit and you can't afford that.

It is easy for a salesperson to say, "Oh sure, I'll take off an extra 15 percent," or, "I'll throw that in." That is not sales! That is cutting profits! You must understand this and so must every one of your employees. Discounting is the surest way to the bottom with the Titanic.

Howard & Phil's had one store with a renegade manager. She discounted to make sales even though it was against company policy. Her store had the highest volume in the chain by a long shot. While it was common knowledge she was discounting, the owners didn't make her stop. When I challenged one of the owner's double standards because they didn't allow any other store managers to discount, the reply to me was, "Bob, high volume hides a wealth of sins." They went bankrupt. Millions of dollars in sales means nothing when there is no profit.

Any student of Accounting 101 can tell you that the profit earned by the average retailer is only one to three cents on the dollar. This fact flies in the face of the common perception that small business owners are raking in the dough. Let's say a bakery serves five hundred customers at an average ticket of $3.00 for a sales total of $1,500 a day. Factor in the cost of employees and materials, lights, rent, insurance, etc. Then take into account burned pastries, spoiled milk and a hundred other seemingly insignificant costs. Do you see how much in sales the retailer needs to sell *just to break even*? How can you even *think* of a buy-one, get-one-free promotion?

Be Ready if an Advertising Bomb Goes Off

The western wear trend began to drop off in the late 80s. I noticed a lot of small western wear stores running large advertisements in the *Los Angeles Times*. They touted some pretty low prices on a limited quantity of their premium goods. Potential customers, lured by their big expensive ads, were disappointed to find when they got to the store that their size was already sold out. Often, I carried the same best-selling items at *my* store. Guess what? I got their disgruntled customers. Time and again they'd say, "The guys down the street have this for half off. Will you match their price?"

With a knowing smile I'd then ask them, "Did they have your size?" They would answer, "No."

I'd reply, "Well if I didn't have something, I'd have it for free."

Usually we'd have a good laugh. I'd explain I had the item, it fit and he could take it home with him right then. Most times it was purchased at my regular retail price.

The competitor's business only got worse as the low prices they charged couldn't cover the steep cost of their advertising. In addition, they lost potential customers drawn by the advertisements who found the shelves empty when they got there. As long as you have trained your salespeople to handle such an event, you'll be fine. When big-box retailers throw a bomb into your operation, if you play your cards right, you might just reap the benefits at your competitor's expense.

Commission Their Sales

While I attended Chapman College, I worked part-time in a shoe store. I'll never forget my first day. I greeted a guy, seated him, took off his shoes, measured his feet and determined his size. I went back and got the shoes for him to try on. I recommended he walk out into the mall a bit to see how they felt. As soon as he was out of earshot, my manager threw a white bottle to me and said, "It cleans and conditions leather. You get 50 cents for each one you sell."

When my customer came back in, I closed the sale and offered to clean his old shoes for free. As I wiped the creme on the shoes, I explained, "This cleans and conditions the leather. If you use it before you polish, you'll see that you get a higher shine and it lasts longer." He bought the cleaner and the polish and I made an extra $1 on that one sale. My daily commission in polishes alone added up nicely.

I know commissions can be hard to manage and may encourage renegades but every person on your floor needs to be commissioned. Commissions are not like a raise or a performance evaluation; either a salesperson has the numbers, or they don't. They are never subjective.

If you are adamantly against commissions, reevaluate your position. If you hate the word commission, consider a drawing, a trip, an extra day off, any incentive that can be tied exclusively to individual sales performance. And even if you already do commissions, a good contest never hurts.

Connect Performance and Tips

Relationship skills are necessary to secure good tips. To be a good server and get those tips, you have to be able to find out what is important to people without them having to tell you beforehand. The server with the highest tips asks *before pouring the coffee* if you want room for cream. The server who sees the bread basket empty and brings another over *without you having to ask for it,* knows this skill well.

I always preface my sales training of servers, people who are typically working towards other careers, by telling them they will be able to use my sales tools in any job. Then I ask, "Why do you think you should care about learning this?" Many fumble for a reason, sometimes giving me what they think I want to hear: the company makes more sales, so the company can pay its bills, so the company makes a profit, so I can keep my job. After a few minutes of this, I take out my wallet and hold it high above my head. Almost immediately several voices shout, "TIPS." "Exactly," I say. "You have the chance to see how good you are at influencing someone every time you wait on a customer. I am not teaching you how to make someone do something they don't want to do. I am teaching you the procedures to be friendly and invitational in a sales situation. If you follow my guidelines, you'll get bigger tips. Period. If you don't do as I say, you won't." At that point they make the connection and they start listening.

An employee who makes the triangle connection between her actions, her customer's satisfaction and profits is someone you can build your business on.

Write Sales Boosters to Combat Boredom

People abandon their jobs because they are bored. Bored by doing the same thing month after month. Bored that every week is not as exciting as Christmas. Bored that there is no change. You must consistently teach people new skills and information if you intend to combat boredom. People who use what they learn should be looked on as having management potential.

Every few weeks I write a sales booster for my clients. It is an easily understandable page that highlights one aspect of the sales process or the features and benefits of a particular product. Sales boosters can be reminders that focus on employee duties. If you notice your store is getting trashy and dirty, you can write one on the importance of everyone maintaining the store's appearance.

You can do this easily. Just make sure you only highlight one aspect. Even if you've said it during training, it isn't so much we need to be taught as much as we need to be reminded. This is a booster I wrote one year:

SALES BOOSTER #10
Hit and Run Greetings with a Prop

Too often salespeople hover or attach themselves to someone right when they walk in. Customers feel smothered and avoid asking anything. They say no, they are just looking. You gain control by the statements you make to them from the outset. Here's how to greet them without scaring them away.

Once you spot a customer looking at all our great stuff, come around the counter with a prop. Walk up to them with a cheerful greeting (that's the hit) and walk away after mentioning something specific about the product they are looking at (that's the run). The prop gives you the reason to leave them. To the customer it looks like you are going to clean something. They won't even have time to get their guard up.

If you see someone milling about in front of the giftware, get over there with a clean up towel and greet them with something like," Welcome to It's A Grind, take a look around, if you have any questions, I'll be right back." Then run along with your prop to something else.

Don't ask if they're finding everything. Instead, walk past them and make a statement about a specific piece of merchandise. An example of a hit-and-run is, We have some different mugs over here with dogs on them. The key is to make statements, not ask questions. That way, no response is required and your customer can't say no.

Remember, don't yell your greeting at a customer from over the counter. Have a destination other than the customer. That's where your prop comes in. The customer will feel more relaxed, feel you are not solely focused on them and eventually be receptive to your suggestions. That way you won't be seen as pushy, just helpful. Then they'll feel they can trust you, even though you hit-and-run.

Although all of It's A Grind's employees had been taught this procedure during training, this sales booster reminded them what was expected in a positive way. Topics of sales boosters frequently include any aspect of the five parts of the sale, customer service and store cleanliness. They can also include new product knowledge, an explanation of new uses for an older product, your reason for adding a new item to your product line, the need your service fills for the customer or even tips from a sales representative.

Sales boosters can address common sales killers. If you have a problem selling expensive leather coats because people say they get rain-spotted easily, come up with a novel approach to address the problem. My quick sales booster would say:

SALES BOOSTER #21
Leather Sales All Wet?

Show your customers how dry and secure they can be in a dramatic demonstration of our water repellant. When the customer has given you the buying sign that they want one of our wonderful leather jackets, they invariably ask, "How will this hold up in the rain?" You answer confidently, "Watch this!"

First, place a small amount of water in the cap of the water repellant. Next come back to the customer while they have the garment on and spray the sleeve lightly with the repellent. Take a small amount of water, pour it over the sleeve of the garment and watch their face as the water beads up and falls on the floor.

Nine out of ten times, you'll not only sell the jacket but a couple of cans of repellent along the way.

We have a leather contest this month, so let's show our customers that leather jackets, properly treated, can leave them high and dry.

Sometimes a sales booster can share something you've learned from an employee with the rest of the crew. Perhaps you get a large percentage of tourists who don't speak English and one employee always seems to be able to work well with them. Have that employee tell you what they do specifically and then write it up in a fun and positive booster.

> As long as people are learning, they're not bored. In order to have things to write about, you have to keep learning new things about your products and your business in general.

Again, you need to know what you are trying to accomplish with the booster so make it like training an employee. Give them an introduction. Tell them what you're going to teach them. Teach them and give an example. Then summarize what you've told them in another way.

No Mental Toothaches Allowed

Employees who come in angry or depressed transfer those feelings directly to the customer. Don't allow it. If you have a toxic person on your floor, find a way for them to be away from your customers and your employees—perhaps it is a good day to reorganize the back room. And whatever you do, don't let employees ever talk about personal problems in front of the customers or guests. Customers who have to hear sob stories are much more inclined to shop elsewhere.

A new employee reminded me of this one day when he stopped outside the store before entering. He said something and then pantomimed heaving something heavy off his back. He then entered the store with a smile. I asked him what all of that was about. He said he was doing like I said and leaving his problems at the door. As he exited that day at the end of his shift, he made a grunting sound. I asked him what was wrong. He said, "Nothing, just my problems are back," and with that he left for home.

While people can have off days, if it becomes a pattern, it is up to you to act decisively before it affects your entire store.

> Anyone in retail is in the hospitality business, not the hostility business.

Ban the Cell Phones!

Stores used to be able to enforce a no personal phone calls policy. But now with the advent of cell phones and pagers, an employee can receive personal phone calls at any place, at any time, even in front of customers. Because these calls often portend bad news, they can take a perfectly happy employee and change him from Dr. Jekyll to Mr. Hyde.

One of the Bay Shores Inn's employees consistently received phone calls from his distraught wife on our phones. From my office I could hear him discussing trivial household matters as if they were major emergencies. He claimed these interruptions didn't bother him but afterwards, when the phone rang with a potential guest, he was suddenly curt. When I told him he couldn't take her calls on our lines, he simply brought in both his pager and cell phone, and the situation got worse until I banned both. I hadn't realized how often he had been distracted until they were gone. Without all the high drama, the atmosphere at the front desk remained calm throughout the day.

Employees are not paid for their problems to be worked out on your phone, on your Internet connection, on their cell phones, or on your payroll.

Cut Employees Loose When They Become a Liability

It was the day before Christmas Eve when I received a complaint about one of my employees again. Hired by a previous manager, Pete had a defiant streak to him; he was a renegade. If you struck him the wrong way, he'd treat you in a very curt, even condescending manner.

In my short time, his behavior warranted two written warnings even though he blamed the customers for the treatment they received.

Then came the call. On one of the busiest days of the year, Pete had chosen to be rude and impertinent to one of the owner's closest friends. This time he couldn't blame his attitude on the customer. I called him into the back room, reminded him we'd had this talk twice before, handed him his check and fired him. He grabbed his stuff and stormed towards the door. He yelled back at me, "Merry F—ing Christmas." I felt bad that it was Christmas Eve, but I knew I'd done the right thing. He had been a liability since the day I got there and I know now that I let him stay too long. Who knows how many customers he'd alienated when I wasn't there to watch him.

When you, your manager or your shift leader feels that an employee has to go, you'd better not allow that employee to still be working there in a week. Part of managing is making the difficult calls in a timely manner.

Create Goals and Make Them Achievable

You need to have a sales goal for your store's crew to see. It must be done before the start of a new month. It could be based on last year's number times a percentage increase. It could be based on the past two months' business. It could be a variation of the two. But it must be reasonable and doable. It cannot be some dreamed up figure that the business has no history doing. Otherwise, it is very defeating. Once you have your goal, break it down into what you need to do each week. Then make adjustments for busier and weaker days.

The employees also needed to know how much they personally had to do to meet their commission goals. Before the month started, I figured out how many hours each person would work and totaled them up. I then divided the store goal by total crew hours. This resulted in the average dollar per hour each employee had to sell. They received a monthly goal based on that formula.

At Howard & Phil's, I created a goal sheet as a visual reminder of each employee's goal and the store goal. The first thing every morning, I took a piece of notebook paper and across the top made columns with every salespersons' name who was working that day. In the right margin, I busted out the daily goal into thirty-minute segments. If I knew we needed to do $3,000 that day, and we were open eleven hours, I divided the $3000 by twenty-two half-hour segments to see that we should be at $136 by 10:30 a.m. I then figured the number of hours the person was scheduled to work. I entered their personal sales goal under their name and placed the sheet on a clipboard next to the register. After ringing up a sale, the employee wrote the total under their name on the sheet. We could all see who was doing what at any time. Several times during the day, I took register readings. I entered the totals next to the time and checked off what we'd achieved in total sales so far.

BOB: $1000	DAVID $800	JERI: $600	TER: $600	VICKI: $300	STORE GOAL: 3128	2/1/01	Reading
45	296	545		35			
100	39	34		109	136	at 10:30 ✓	
$145	335	579		244	272	at 11 ✓	
697	79				408	at 11:30 ✓	
842	414				544	at Noon✓	$690
					580	at 12:30 ✓	
					816	at 1	
					952	at 1:30	
					1088	at 2	
					1224	2:30	
					1360	at 3	
					1496	at 3:30	$725
					1632	at 4	$2079
					1768	at 4:30	
					1904	at 5	
					2040	at 5:30	
					2176	at 6	
					2312	at 6:30	
					2448	at 7	
					2584	at 7:30	
					2720	at 8	
					2856	at 8:30	
					3000	at 9	

In the above example, you can see that the crew had already hit 12:30 p.m.'s goal by noon. However, we weren't on pace to hit our 4 p.m. goal when a 3:30 rush hit. Suddenly we could all see that we were again on pace to make our daily goal.

This sheet served as a great motivator.

During the holidays, on particularly high volume days, I'd break out the super high goals into as little as fifteen-minute segments to make each goal more manageable to look at. Inch by inch goal making's a cinch.

Hold Employees Accountable—The Shark Chart

At the end of each day, I took each employee's sales total and divided it by the hours they'd worked. This gave me their sales per hour. I then entered this on my Shark Chart, a graph I created at the beginning of each month. The Shark Chart is simple, the days of the month across the bottom, ascending numbers in units of two or three dollars on the left side and a legend showing each employee in a different color. Take the average dollar per hour everyone in the store has to sell, and draw a heavy line at the corresponding dollar value. This should be about 3/4 of the way up from the bottom. About midway, I drew a big fin coming out of the water, like *Jaws*. On the chart I placed a corresponding dot each day for each employee's daily hourly sales average. By connecting the dots, it became obvious who was doing the job and who wasn't. I posted it where everyone could see it on a daily basis.

The Shark Chart was something everyone looked at and commented on. And don't think it didn't put pressure on me. I had to lead by example and be at the top.

If it became clear I had an employee with a pattern of being underwater much of the time, I took them aside and explained that we needed to get their head above water. I offered to work with them on an individual basis.

Many times though, they couldn't cut it and, like human shark bait, were gone fairly quickly. Shark Charts are a great way to hold people accountable for their sales in an easy-to-read format that lets almost everyone have fun. Although I used to use graph paper, I now recommend that you do this on Excel or another computer program. You can find great shark clip art to spice it up. The Shark Chart will help you highlight your top salespeople and help you motivate the others.

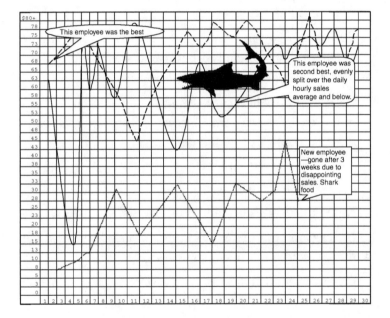

I always heard other salespeople say I was *just lucky* or that my customers came in *ready to buy*. They never thought I did anything extraordinary. I had to find a way to share what I did with my crew and show them there were concrete ways to becoming top salespeople. Where ever I went, the following twelve steps hung on my wall. They served as a model and showed that extraordinary sales were within anyone's reach.

The Retail Doctor's Twelve Steps To Being Top Salesperson

1. Maintain a positive attitude towards yourself and your work. When something goes wrong, don't waste time complaining but work towards its correction.

2. Understand a clean and organized store directly correlates to high sales.

3. Approach more customers.

4. Realize that customers are on the defensive. Make a personal remark that demands a positive answer, putting the customer at ease. Never say, "Can I help you?"

5. Carry a prop when approaching a customer and get away quickly to let the customer browse. Return within a few minutes and continue to build rapport.

6. Ask questions that open windows; rarely ask anything that can be answered with a *no*.

7. Know the store's stock and don't oversell limited items.

8. Never come out of the stockroom empty-handed. If something is sold out, present something similar.

9. Present additional products and accessories at the close of the sale.

10. Locate out-of-stock items from other stores or suggest special ordering other alternatives. Take a deposit to ensure the customer really wants the item.

11. Understand the merchandise: its price points, construction, wear and how it compares to other brands and competitors. Ask about new products before a customer does.

12. Thank customers *by name* at the time of sale and again with a short note the following day.

CHAPTER **9**

Your Face to the World
MARKETING

"It's not that the big will overtake the small, it's the creative that will devour the passive."

N ow that your facility is in shape and your salespeople are trained and ready for business, it is finally time to market. Marketing doesn't exist in a vacuum; it is just one component of the triangle that, like sales and facility, supports a successful operation.

Do Your Homework—How to Sell Your Image
Know if You Are a Want or a Need Business

Most retailers will acknowledge that they are in the *people* business. They remember that sales are based on a relationship

If you don't think you need to market your business, you're dead wrong. Someone else already is: the chain stores.

between employees and customers. That's obvious. What is often *not* obvious is whether their success is based on what people *want* or *need*.

The *want* retailer must see that most of what they carry has a certain *cachet* that makes it a *want* item; something that, with a bit of salesmanship and merchandising, will give a special feeling to the buyer. *This item is handmade by local artisans* or *this wine is one of a select vintage from a three hundred year old vintner* or *our soup-of-the-day was made from vegetables picked from our garden.* You get my point.

No one *needs* a $5 specialty espresso drink. No one *needs* a $230 room at the beach when the freeway-close Motel 6 has a bed. No one *needs* a fancy day-spa treatment when a hot bath in your own tub can relax you. No one needs a fancy window treatment for $1,500.

However, if you own the specialty coffeehouse, the bed & breakfast, the health resort, or the window covering dealer, you'd better have the words necessary to make the customer want it. We all enjoy the extravagance of buying things we *want* but don't need. If you can't make your merchandise sound better and put it in a class by itself, you undoubtedly will not get a premium price for it. You will be reduced to sale banners and coupons.

Notice that the flower shop who says *We provide a wealth of floral related gifts under fifty dollars for corporate accounts* is in a much stronger position to market than one who says *We are a florist.* The first would seek out advertising vehicles to target their business customers. Is there anything clear about what customer *We are a florist* is seeking? No. They will try lots of things in hopes of addressing *someone's* need, rather than trying a few targeted appeals to attract their special niche. The first will selectively mail the newest, prettiest gifts for the holiday season to a prescreened list with suggestions showing how they can be personalized with corporate logos. The second shop will take out an ad and put up a matching banner in front of their store screaming *Dozen roses for $19.99.*

If the second shop had discovered who they were and who their customers were, they might have put up a different banner that simply said, *Make somebody else's day better than yours was—we deliver*. No price, just an appeal to the want of making someone else feel special.

Know Who You Are and Develop a Plan

Clever marketing starts with a clear identity of who you are and who you aren't. An identity is not that you carry a screwdriver set, or a cup of coffee, or a tangle-free rinse for your shaggy dog. A clear identity answers the question, *What makes you unique?*

Picture the following scenario. You are entering an elevator and someone follows you in. He or she is a potential customer, vendor or referral. They ask, "So what do you do?" As you go up the elevator, you have four quick floors to tell them about your business. If you are still talking as they exit the elevator, they are probably still unsure what you do. Maybe that's because you've never had to put down in words what you do. Now is the time.

Begin by taking a legal pad of paper and writing words that describe your business. You are looking for things that define the identity of your store. This brainstorming technique is a place to develop as many ideas as you can. Don't judge or correct them. You may even want your employees to help.

After you've come up with your list, prioritize it. Each time you think, *yes that's us*, put a star by the word or words. Please don't say *we provide great service*. It's like saying *we have clean rooms* in a hotel. We already take that as a given and it makes us wonder why you felt you had to say it. Service is something that has to be demonstrated. Period.

Once you have gone through your list, put it away and come back to it the following week. Repeat the star procedure. Remember you're looking for an *a-ha* moment. Throw away all but the top-five starred items. What you have left should be a good idea of who you are. In short, you've found your identity.

From those five items should come two ideas that can be combined into one powerful, concise statement. When you read it, you instantly go *a-ha—that's us*. Such a statement might be *We provide the best damn coffee in Lubbock in a friendly and relaxed atmosphere.* It might be *Our team excels at finding the perfect curtains for country kitchens worldwide.* But it has to come from YOU and your store.

When people ask me what I do, I answer, "I help small and medium sized independent businesses succeed—especially when they are threatened by chain stores." Is there any question of my business?

I was on a radio talk show a few months back and a woman called in with a problem. She and her husband owned a company that made airplane parts and sales were going down. What could they do? I asked her my standard question, "What makes your product better than the other guy's?"

After a moment she answered, "Nothing." I told her that was probably her biggest problem. If she didn't know what made her better, how the heck could a customer know?

Once you have a good idea of who you are and what you offer, you can build a framework for all of your marketing choices. That framework tells you where to put your money and time, what extra services to offer and most importantly, what kind of marketing materials to use and to avoid.

There is a clever way to hone in on your specialty; it takes brainstorming, patience and creativity. When you think you've got it, try it out on your customers. Ask them if it sounds like you and your business; if so, proceed. If not, keep trying until you get it right.

You can continue to improve your business by developing an advertising campaign, a plan of action for *every month*. That way, you will be ahead of deadlines and have a regular presence in the mind of your customers.

Don't get overwhelmed with the task; you just need something in writing that lists how you will communicate with both existing and new customers. Like a good news story, your advertising campaign or marketing plan simply includes who, what, when, where, why and how.

Know Who Your Customer Is and Isn't

By scanning your mailing list, you are bound to discover a majority of your business comes from a certain area.

I was intrigued to learn that the Bay Shores Inn drew a majority of its guests from two cities, Las Vegas and Phoenix. Yet common knowledge in the hospitality industry is that most people drive no more than two hours for a weekend trip. If I had gone only by that information, I never would have advertised in Las Vegas or Phoenix. I would have blown my advertising dollars in northern Los Angeles or San Diego.

By looking at Polly's Gourmet Coffee's mailing list and talking with customers, I found a high percentage of them owned their own homes and lived within walking distance of the store. But I wanted to expand my knowledge and find out how many people in our neighborhood shopped at Polly's. Since they had been in business for over twenty years, I figured that everyone in the neighborhood already knew who Polly's was.

One day I took samples of fresh roasted coffee, attached a flier and visited 500 homes in the immediate area. I was amazed to find that 30 percent of the residents in Polly's own neighborhood didn't even know where Polly's Gourmet Coffee was located!

With that disturbing information, I went to the library where the public records showed that in a two-year period, the neighborhood's home ownership had changed 50 percent. That meant Polly's Gourmet Coffee would have an entirely new customer base about every four years! And that was just the homeowners; I didn't even factor in the rental units.

The results of visiting those homes and the library helped me establish the basis for Polly's marketing plan. I couldn't count on name recognition, Polly's needed to actively have its name out there as if it were a new company.

You need to know, in as much detail as you can, who your customers are and where they come from. What age are they? What's their education level? Are they generally single or married? Do they generally have kids? Do the men generally own their own businesses? Do they collect art or craft? What kind of cars do they drive? Do they travel much or belong to your local country club? Compile your own list.

When I first met Bryan Johnson at Haute Links in Lake Forest, CA, I asked him who his customers were. "Pretty evenly split with all types," is what Bryan guessed. Yet while I was standing there, 80 percent of the people in line were guys! When I brought this to Bryan's attention, he was genuinely surprised.

No marketing can be truly effective without specific customer information. In Bryan's case, I crafted his advertising to fit the young, professional guys who worked for the big technology companies that surrounded him.

Unsure of who your market is? Look around your store and poll your customers. As the owner, you can do this informally through your personal conversations, or you can staple a brief survey to every bag and offer a reward for returning it.

After defining your customer base, you can look for ways to expand it. If your clientele is mostly housewives looking for casual clothes, a brochure that focuses on short skirts and low-cut tops probably won't appeal to them. If men are considering your store and they see mostly women's items in your ads, they won't come in. Like attracts like.

Focus yourself down to the clients who've used you in the past. Don't use anecdotal evidence. Sure it may be interesting that a young woman with pink hair, a *U2 Rocks* tattoo on her neck and a plaid jumpsuit walked into your store. But unless you see lots of women like her, don't include her. If your customers are hip-hop kids under twenty, then expand that base.

With the profile, you can decide where your marketing money is best spent and how to reach more of your target customers.

> Without a customer profile, you are taking a shotgun to the air and hoping it hits something.

Focus Your Advertising on Your Target Audience

You don't market to the smallest niche of your customers in hopes of growing that business. For example, if tea drinkers make up less than 1 percent of your drink sales, don't commit money to an ad campaign in hopes of increasing tea sales. Even if you double your percentage, you still only have 2 percent. The money it took to advertise wasn't worth the return. Plan wisely. Find the bait to attract the swarm, not an occasional bee.

The big-boxes often make their ads generic and interchangeable no matter the locale. None of them take into account the individual neighborhoods their stores are located in. Think Lowe's and Home Depot. Think J. Crew and Banana Republic. Think Sears and J.C. Penney. Think McDonald's and Starbucks. One size fits all.

The independents' advantage over these big chains is that they know their neighborhoods and their customers. With a little time and money, they can speak directly and creatively to *just* them.

Image Ads

I am a big believer in image ads. Image ads do not include a price or necessarily a product. They frequently are just text or a photograph. Think of Ralph Lauren. Their ads might feature a sailboat filled with beautifully dressed women and men with just the words Ralph Lauren at the bottom. This designer is advertising a lifestyle, not a specific product. Because people like that image, it is expected they will want to dress to fit it.

The image advertisements that I come up with all have a narrow point of view, a focus and humor. These ads are intended to get across an image, a feeling and a warm fuzzy or smile that links the brand with the reader's response.

Good marketing of an image, like good sales skills, is nothing more than what? *A transference of feeling.* Think White Diamonds or Obsession. Think Coca-Cola or Mountain Dew. Think Gap or Calvin Klein. All of these use various lifestyles to market their image.

As a small retailer, you too have the option to create a powerful image campaign.

Clever Ads Make Us Ask, *Who Is This?*

The best ads make you want to know *whose ad is this?* Consider the Nike sports commercials; they always end with a black screen and the swoosh. Based on the strength of that swoosh, they no longer mention Nike. Or consider the Target print ads with a large photo of the item they are featuring, some miniature person looking at it and a small Target logo at the bottom right corner of the ad. We are intrigued and our curiosity is satisfied.

The image ads I created for Polly's Gourmet Coffee always got people talking. I rarely used graphics, just text with a humorous follow-up and the logo. I wanted the ad to quickly create an extraordinary moment, an inner chuckle that would link good feelings with Polly's Gourmet Coffee.

A Best Western image ad campaign featured a series of three television commercials. Each began with an immediate attention grabber and ended with a blue screen and logo. One featured a close-up of a grandmother type preparing to dive off a waterfall in Hawaii. Another featured a man escorting a blind man to the edge of the Grand Canyon. Both were strong images that made us wonder and wait for the ending. They had a point, a vision and a message that transcended the need to put heads in beds, and they all ended with the tag line: *For every reason to travel there's a Best Western.*

The third ad took place in a big office where the chief tells an assistant he has to go to Wichita the next day. The assistant smiles to the boss but then passes it off to another and then he passes it off to someone lower until we finally see a man asking the young man at the copier, "You ever been to Wichita?" The next frame was just text, *Because someone's got to go* followed by the same tag line. It was great!

To Ordinary You're A "Tall Drip"

To Us You're A Neighbor

Wakin' up Belmont Shore with fresh roasted coffee since 1976
4606 E. 2nd St.
www.pollys.com

Down The Street From Ordinary(s)

Little Know Fact: The Borg Started in Seattle

POLLY'S GOURMET COFFEE

Wakin' up Belmont Shore with fresh roasted coffee since 1976
4606 E. 2nd St.
www.pollys.com

Down The Street From Ordinary(s)

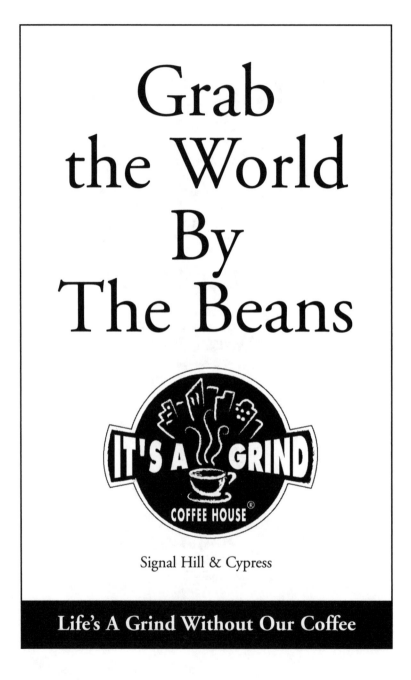

Survivor
Shouldn't refer to your TV set

Screens have gotten a lot bigger and clearer. See what you've been missing.

Sony 42" with remote

Epic Touch
Elkhart
451 Morton
620-697-2233

Bringing the World to Elkhart Since 1958

Beware of trying to copy someone else's image. Clever for one business is not necessarily clever for another. The California Milk Advisory Board hired a witty ad agency who came up with the award winning ad campaign *Got milk?* It was simple, to the point and lent itself to great advertising both on TV and in print; it was brilliant. Unfortunately, many people decided they too were clever if they just changed the last word. A host of knockoffs have been seen including *Got church? Got dirt? Got trains? Got gifts?* Don't copy others; you run the risk of looking generic. Use your own creativity to promote what makes you unique.

Use a Card File to Hold on to Current Customers

There is nothing that develops loyalty as much as sending personal notes to customers expressing your appreciation of their business. Written thank you notes are the way to make *word-of-mouth* marketing happen. Everyone likes to be noticed.

> It takes three to five times as much money to get a new customer than it does to keep an old one.

When I became became responsible for a store in Santa Monica, I was faced with a daunting challenge. The store had one of the highest goals in the company, yet due to poor previous management, they had the lowest prospects for success. All of the stores were having a big invitation-only customer sale at the end of the month. Success for each store was dependent on having a large mailing list. Santa Monica's mailing list was almost nonexistent. I had to get names and develop relationships on my own—fast.

With each customer, all of the employees had to fill out an information card that contained the customer's name and address and noted what they had purchased. During the quiet times the following morning, I sent out a note to those who had spent more than $100 the previous day, referring to exactly what they bought and offering a suggestion for care. I also enclosed a business card. With those names I began to grow a huge mailing list.

I had one customer come back and spend nearly $5,000 with me in the course of that first month. When I asked him why he came back, his answer was simple. "Your note reminded me of the good time I had when I was here and I decided to come back and visit you. I've never gotten a card from any store before," he said. He referred his friends to me and before I knew it, I was the top store.

Recently, as part of a *Los Angeles Times* business makeover, I suggested that Jackie Robinson, a leather designer in Malibu, write three notes to her new customers. She would send the first note out after she received the down payment. It would thank the customer for the order, say how much she was looking forward to creating it and assure them they would stand out in a garment that was personally designed for them. The second note was to be sent after the customer had taken delivery of their garment. It would say what a pleasure it had been to create the outfit and include a tip about care. A third was to be sent out with a couple of business cards a month after the customer had taken delivery. It would express how much she hoped they were enjoying their purchase and request they pass her card along to anyone who could use her services.

Is holding on to your customers with thank you notes expensive? No. Is it a key to an independent's survival? Absolutely. Why? Because your customers are made to feel special in their homes. Anyone can appreciate the time and consideration it takes to do such a thing. And personal notes always get opened—not tossed in the trash along with the 10 percent off coupons from other retailers. In addition, customers comment on them when they see you next, sometimes even coming in again just to thank *you*!

If you don't feel comfortable writing notes and thank you cards yourself, have an employee who can write legibly do it. Much like a script, give them a template of what you want to say: "Dear _____, Just a quick note to thank you for _____." Add a sentence unique to your wares and then inspect them before they go out.

The Bay Shores Inn sends out a picture postcard of Newport Beach to anyone who spends two or more nights. That card is just another reminder of the great time they had. That's one reason why sales have doubled since I came on board; thank you notes make your business memorable.

Reward Your Customers

Find a way to reward those loyal customers on your mailing list. If you are a coffeehouse or retail clothing store, start a frequent buyer club. At a plumbing supply, a simple addition to your billing program offers a free widget-of-the-month or credit to those customers who purchase a set amount of merchandise. Any reward you give that features your logo is even better. It's not important what you do as long as you keep finding ways to reward loyal customers.

It's A Grind Coffee sent out postcards offering a free decal with any purchase of one of their new drinks. More than 10 percent of their mailing list responded to the give-away. Now when you drive around Long Beach, you can spot their customers advertising It's A Grind.

Get Old Customers to Come Back

Consider a person who goes to a restaurant and has a great time. They tell friends about it for a day or two. Friends telling friends about a business is again the core of word-of-mouth advertising. After a short time though, their experience and connection to your restaurant is pretty much forgotten. Years may pass before someone says to them, *You ever been to ...?* and the original person's memory is jogged. The astute restaurateur will find a way to get them to come back with a postcard about new menu selections, special events or even a personal call or note.

Successful independent retailers should send each person at a certain buying level on their mailing list at least one personal note a year. Arrange your list alphabetically by last name and each week send a small part of the list a note. For example, send all the A's a note during the first week of January, all the B's the second week, etc. For larger lists the task is more daunting but you probably have more staff to spread the workload around.

> Successful independent retailers should send each person at a certain buying level on their mailing list at least one personal note a year.

Your note must be simple. Begin with, *Hi _____(their first name)!* If you are a retail clothing store, continue with *I just got some new arrivals I think you might like.* If you are a women's shoe store, you might say *We are having a trunk show by your favorite designer in two weeks.* If you are a kid's bookstore you might continue with *We're having a tea party and I thought Jenny would like to come and play dress-up. It would be great to see you both again.*

These are not printed cards that you just sign. These are hand-written cards personal and personalized.

Whatever your system and message, the desired effect is to keep in touch with old customers and find ways to keep them coming back on a regular basis. Even when there is a problem, you can get customers to come back.

A friend of mine told me about a bad experience she had at a local bakery. She had ordered one of their custom cakes for a very special dinner party she was having. When she went in to pick up the cake, she was told they couldn't take her check. Seems the particular bank charged the merchant to verify funds. It was the owner's goal to have the customers complain to the bank so the bank could see the error of their ways. It backfired.

My friend left without her cake and her dinner party was ruined.

She told everyone about her negative experience. That was eight years ago.

Recently, I was asked by the owners to
consult about their business. I relayed the
story to them and they asked for my friend's
name and address. To their credit, they took
immediate action and sent her a cookie in
the shape of a dog bone. The creative card

> A Simple Truth:
> Treat people
> well and they'll
> be your best
> advocates.

said, *Come in and chew us out.* A $25 gift certificate was enclosed.
Even after eight years, they got her and her friends back.

Ask for Testimonials and Referrals

Referrals from satisfied customers transfer their good feelings about
you to potential new customers. Painting contractors, accountants,
custom furniture makers, floor covering companies and tailors are
but a few of the many that are helped immensely by positive testimonials from people who have used their services.

To facilitate referrals, design a short postcard and send it out to
your satisfied customers asking for their recommendation and permission to use their name for a referral list. Sound easy? It is.

After you have a few responses, organize them by city and include
their comments on one sheet of paper. Whenever you find yourself
with a skeptical buyer, you can say something like, "Mrs. Smith had
the same concerns and she was so satisfied, she agreed to be on my
referral list. If you'd like to have her tell you about what I did, here's
her number." That would go a long way to alleviating your buyer's
skepticism. Plus once they like your job, they'll be happy to do the
same for someone else.

Business referrals payoff has no expiration date if you did the job
well. You may be surprised when you ask someone how they heard
about you and they answer *someone you laid a floor for ten years earlier had referred me to you.*

When Molly Pratt began selling real estate in 1956, she always arranged to be at her clients' new home to have the gas turned on, the phone number changed and the electricity switched over, all before the homeowner took possession. When she handed over the keys, Molly also made sure they had her business card. Then, every few years she also sent them a personal note. That connection with the homeowners lasted for thirty-plus years. She sold more homes in her seventies than she ever sold when she was younger. When it came time for these homeowners, their friends or their children to buy or sell a home, there was really only one person to refer them to, Molly Pratt.

Develop a Customer Database

Because people move more often, you need to find new names to replace those who have moved away from your shop. Take anything you have with your customer's name, address and phone number and enter them into a computer database like Access or Excel. Include columns where you check off how and when you contacted them. Additional columns could include the last time you saw them, what they purchased and any wants they may have expressed but didn't buy.

Consider a contest; customers love to win things. I encourage all of my clients to find ways to have at least two contests a year. Prizes have ranged from cash to trips to toys but they all have the same goal, to get customers' names. Use this to your advantage by creating the drawing slips with spaces for name, address and zip code. At the bottom of the slip print *Winner notified by mail only*.

Encourage customers to send in photos of themselves in your clothes with your slogan. You will want a story of where the photo was taken. Winners get a prize and you get unique photos for display and use in your mailings. Because entries come with return addresses, you will get more names for your mailing list and another fun opportunity to contact your customers.

I offered such a contest at the Bay Shores. People had to take a picture of themselves in an exotic location with a sign that said *Stay at the Bay Shores Inn in Newport Beach, CA.* We received photos from the Florida Keys and other exotic tropical locales. We even had photos taken in an operating room complete with doctors in surgical garb! The winning photo was taken after an April snowstorm in the upper Midwest. A young girl, all bundled up for the cold, is stretched out on a towel in the snow. Around her were a beach ball, the sign and a beach umbrella. Her family won two free nights at the hotel. It was a great success.

Take the names and addresses off of every check you take as payment in your store. Consider having a guest book for visitors; it could even have a place where satisfied customers can write in their own testimonials. The important thing is to get the names of people who know you and your shop, and then keep in touch.

Do Your Homework : How to Sell Your Product

Build Partnerships
If your cater to the top 5 percent income bracket, find other successful retailers and servicers in your area who cater to that same clientele. Create advertising that links your businesses and then send it to your joint mailing lists.

As an elite retailer, look for the jeweler where the customer designs their own custom jewelry. Pursue the store where a man has his shirts custom-made for him. Search out the prominent car dealer who does an exceptional job at servicing his clients. The idea is to look at the whole life of your customer and find as many like interests to cross-reference as possible.

One great four-color brochure where several merchants have shared expenses is potentially worth far more than your limited one-store finances can afford. Malls know this and selectively invite established merchants who share similar customer profiles to band together. The independent can do this as well with great results, and it works for all levels of income earners.

A hardware store can form a partnership with a local nursery, lighting store and craft store and then create a flier that cross promotes the businesses. They can offer display space in each other's stores from time to time. They can sponsor joint classes at all three businesses titled *How to create the perfect garden*. The classes could include how to landscape, illuminate, irrigate and personalize an outdoor garden.

Whatever your business, synergy comes from partnering with people and businesses that have common interests and clients.

Form Alliances with Your Competitors
After you've explored partnerships with businesses who do not directly compete with yours, explore how such a partnership would work between you and your competitors. Such an alliance offers cost savings and increased exposure for both businesses. It is a rare business that is

identical to the other in terms of location, product and ambiance.

Not long into my relationship with the Bay Shores Inn, I realized that none of the small inns in the area were cross-selling their properties. I obtained rates, amenities, and specific features and benefits for each establishment and made up a spreadsheet to be used at the front desk at each of the seven properties. That way, when one inn was sold out, they could refer to the spreadsheet and suggest alternatives to the guest. The customer wins in such a deal because they find lodging, the city wins because the tax revenue stays in Newport Beach, the property that was referred gets business they wouldn't have gotten, and the business who was full loses nothing but gains favor from the inn they referred.

I also came up with the idea of building a brochure to feature just the small inns and bed and breakfasts in Newport Beach. The Newport Beach Visitor and Convention Bureau now hands out this brochure whenever someone wants information about Newport Beach in general or as a potential conference site.

Sales for all the inns have gone up and stayed up. That partnership still exists and is a great example of how similar businesses can align themselves to gain more clout, more visibility and greater sales.

In 1999, I started an alliance among three of the best-known coffeehouses in Long Beach. This was framed to the media as the small guys getting together to challenge the big chains. Each member pays an equal portion of a joint ad campaign that includes each business's logo. The alliance is also looking at how they can join together to cater large events, do donations as a group for local charities and even hold an annual golf tournament to benefit the local Fire Department. The alliance entered a float in the local holiday parade gaining face-to-face exposure to over 60,000 people. The float cost over $5,000, something a single retailer could not afford, but as part of an alliance, it was a prize-winning success.

If you have a hardware store, build alliances with other independent hardware stores in your town. Personally call on the owner and be able to clearly tell them how your alliance will add to their business. The shortsighted will think you are out to steal their customers. The smart will recognize that when one store doesn't have an item, it will benefit all the small retailers if another small retailer makes the sale. Aggressively promote such an alliance.

Remember that the professionals who frequent your store—the contractors, builders, electricians, plumbers and landscapers probably have jobsites both near and far, oftentimes many miles away from your store. If they are too far from your store while on a job, they might be tempted to shop with the big-box stores because they don't know another independent hardware store exists closeby. Advertising as an alliance solves this problem and keeps all of those professionals shopping with the independents.

This point was particularly well highlighted in the 1947 holiday classic, *Miracle on 34th St.* when Macy's Santa recommended other stores—even archrival Gimbals. The top management at first was outraged and then saw the sales numbers and public sentiment rise. It's not fiction; when one wins in an alliance, everyone wins.

Lead with Your Strengths

Every business has one product area that sells well and its advertising should concentrate on that area. Advertise the product that most of your customers already want, the one that has the most potential for lifting your store's total volume. Don't advertise the least desirable, least profitable or most unusual product or service you offer.

If your hardware store sells a ton of keys during the year, make that a focus of your ads. But as I said earlier, if you are tempted to create a key ad because you want to increase your key sales from 1 percent, pass. Even if you double sales, you still are left with a marginal increase in the total performance of your store. However, if you sell only a few lawn mowers, but they make up 25 percent of your total spring sales, advertising them would be the best use of your money.

The Bay Shores Inn is a twenty-five room hotel nestled between Balboa Bay and the Pacific Ocean. The Balboa Peninsula is often referred to as the California Riviera and is one of the finest neighborhoods on the coast. All of the Bay Shores advertisements highlight the bed & breakfast ambiance and ideal location. Since the property's strengths are its location and relaxed atmosphere, we don't want to advertise its standard amenities like cable TV, private parking or air-conditioned rooms.

If 85 percent of your clientele's money is spent on iced espresso drinks, advertise this favorite to your local market. If you also happen to carry ice cream, have your point-of-purchase (POP) advertise that in-store, but don't commit big money to outside ads. The ice cream is something people who know you will come in for during the summer, but your main business year-round is the espresso drink.

If your nursery sells mostly colorful seasonal bedding plants, advertise that to your local market. While you also carry the tools, realize they are something your salespeople should be suggesting. If you sell a majority of murder mysteries in your bookstore, don't advertise the few cookbooks you might have. Save them for a small inclusion in a holiday mailer to the customers on your mailing list.

Product Ads
A good product ad is more than a picture or an item with a price. Because it will take more than a picture to bring customers to your store, your ad needs words to energize, intrigue and grab the reader. A product ad often includes the details of ingredients, how it is made and the benefits to the customer. Perhaps it is new to the marketplace, a return of an old favorite, or some item that is especially hot that you want to make sure everyone knows you have.

For Polly's Thanksgiving season, I created a product ad that featured a *Thanksgiving Survival Kit.*

The humorous words linked our product to a situation everyone could relate to.

What you are advertising could also highlight special features and benefits. Link the picture with words that tell how great this item will look in the home, in the car or on your customer; how it will intrigue, relax or energize the customer; or simplify, accessorize or compliment their environment.

Not sure what to write? Call your manufacturers for any printed materials they might have; the smart ones will have done the bulk of the work for you and may even provide camera-ready ad slicks.

One last thing about product print ads, don't overwhelm the reader with an inordinate amount of information; a little goes a long way. Find the one, most compelling feature and benefit. Take no more than two sentences to say it. Choose a simple font. Include the price only if you think there is great value in it.

Remember, higher end goods carry more of a cachet and are designed to be *wants* not *needs*. Creative advertising peaks our interest in these higher priced goods. Once the customer arrives at your door, they must be met by a well-trained crew who can build on the excitement your ad created. Only with that follow-up can you be sure your hard work pays off.

You've Done Your Homework—Now Sell Yourself Brand Your Customers

Only two soft drinks dominate the world market, Coca-Cola and Pepsi. Why is that? Because both companies spend billions of dollars in advertising so that you never forget they are there. They have POP materials that feature their logo all over retailers' stores; they are in the video rental aisles, on billboards, on the radio, in the movies and on the Internet. They are everywhere. Much like cattle, we have been branded as their property, and we respond by purchasing their products.

Big-box retailers know this too well. Their national brands are quickly recognized in any town. They convey a message of consistency and that is the precise reason they are such a threat to the independent. Whether we are in Budapest or Boston, we know what to expect when we see a McDonald's. In your own marketplace, you and your advertising must be just as recognizable.

As an independent, you don't have the resources to compete against a massive marketing campaign like Coke, Pepsi or McDonald's, but you can still get your logo on everything. If you don't have a great logo, hire a local graphic artist to make one for you that is unique and easily identifiable. From your napkins, to your drink cups, from your outside signage to your sugar packets, from your pens to your brochures—any time you order a supply for your business, logo it!

When I started with Polly's, Mike Sheldrake was using styrofoam cups. Because they were the generic cheap cups you find at any restaurant supply house, they directly contradicted the image of a superior product. I quickly found a cup that could be custom printed.

Then I created a contest for local artists to submit their designs, all using Polly's Gourmet Coffee logo. Within two months we had about a dozen entries for our panel of judges which included a local businessperson, the head of the university graphic art department and a representative from the local arts council. Rather than choose just one of the top designs, we chose to utilize the top three designs, one each on the small, medium and large coffee cups. The community loved them! The cups put Polly's name out there, aligned us as supporting local artists and they looked great. Now Polly's Gourmet Coffee logo goes out the door 500 times a day and keeps the brand fresh in people's minds.

When the *Los Angeles Times* asked me to do a business makeover for Haute Links, I told owner Bryan Johnson that he had to stop packaging his takeout gourmet sausage sandwiches in cheap supermarket-type plastic bags. He now has a kraft bag that says, "Inside: delicious sausage sandwiches with half the fat and calories." At the bottom is his redesigned logo and a new tag phrase, "Sausage sandwiches that are probably healthier than you are." Those takeout orders, like small billboards, carry his logo back to offices all over Orange County and his sales have risen dramatically.

When I began working with Marty Cox of It's A Grind, he had those A-frame plywood sandwich-board signs in front of his coffeehouses. Each sign listed three or four products, the hours of operation and the name of his business. I had the signs remade with only two elements, a huge version of his three-color logo and a bright red arrow below. Now, this heightened visibility of his logo easily catches the eye of speeding drivers.

Reminder: never have more than one logo. While you can have a color and a black and white version, the basic logo must remain the same.

Develop Materials that Speak to Your Customers

Every store needs POP materials that support the personality and image you have created in your advertising. Your price lists, special offers and fliers must all be seen as part of your marketing efforts.

Therefore, make your POP materials peak our interest. The customer must be able to do a quick scan of them and get the main points at once. Don't detail everything possible about your product or service; you'll end up with most of the information presented in too small a type—nothing will stand out. Should they desire further details, your POP materials should include your website and your store phone number.

Create a Unique Slogan

Create a tag line that sets you apart. At Polly's I chose the underdog image and my desire to define our competition and their product in my terms. This resulted in *Down the Street From Ordinary* which spoke to the fact that we were special and down the street from Starbucks, which for coffee, has become as ordinary as McDonald's for many people. The second year, I added (s) to the slogan to make an additional reference to the fact that there were now two Starbucks within ten blocks of the store.

Down the Street From Ordinary (s) has been on every ad, POP, newsletter, commercial, flier, contest, radio and sponsorship we have done since. Consistency is what it is all about. You don't want to change a tag line in midstream. It will continue to underscore the image of who you are for years to come, long after you've become tired of it.

Use Business Cards

A business card is a small billboard. Carry them with you. Make sure they truly represent what you do. Like other POP materials, your business card must be a quick-read with crucial information gleaned in one brief look. Make your card stand out with a clear, concise message either in text or with a photograph, that anyone can grasp quickly.

One of my clients was a woman who marketed Hispanic events. The first day we met, she presented her card to me. I was confused. At the top was a nautical flag. When I asked why it was there, she proudly told me that it meant service. I was floored. "And how does this relate to who you are and who your clientele is?" I asked. "Are there many Hispanic boat owners in your market? Do most of your clients know how to read nautical flags?" Then I told her to get new cards.

It is not enough to have compelling and focused business cards unless you carry them with you at all times and look for ways to get them into people's hands. When I consulted with Jackie Robinson at Leather Waves she told me she ran into her former client Goldie Hawn in a restaurant. Goldie said she wanted some new outfits and asked for a card. Jackie had none and had just moved—she hasn't seen Goldie again.

Create a Newsletter

One of the best places to market yourself is in a newsletter you create and mail to your own customers. You can tell your story more completely, and the people reading it should have more than a passing interest in what it says. Page one might include how you started or why you do what you do. Inside is a great space to explain free workshops, seminars and classes. If you have a children's bookstore, a coloring contest for kids might be appropriate to include along with storytelling times, the latest bestsellers and a parents' guidebook. A hotel's newsletter might include places to visit with dates, times and places of upcoming special events in the city and a number to call for further information. A gourmet food retailer could include recipes, an explanation of the origin of certain utensils or information on particular spices.

> Tip: to keep customers reading through your newsletter, continue a front-page story onto page three.

A great newsletter must include lots of graphics. Keep your margins large and your type size no smaller than 11 pt. Keep it a quick read. Most word processing software already have templates you can customize. Tip: to keep customers reading through your newsletter, continue a front-page story onto page three.

As with any mailed promotion, make sure you have enough lead time to get your newsletter into the hands of the intended readers. Work back from the date you want it to be there to allow for the mailing house (or your staff) to label and stamp it, the printer to produce it (usually two weeks) and your time to write and proof it (a month on this step alone is standard).

Use Fliers

Fliers in newspapers, on cars or handed out on the street to people who don't know you are a waste of time and money.

However, fliers used in-store are an inexpensive way to highlight specific promotions at a fraction of the newsletter's cost. Fliers are aimed at people who are not on your mailing list, and the information they contain is oftentimes similar if not directly lifted from your newsletter. While the standard flier is 8 1/2 x 11, half sheets can do quite nicely and result in twice as many fliers for the same price. Keep it simple. Answer the who, what, when, where and why quickly; then add your logo and slogan and run them off on a copy machine. Have enough on hand for your customers to give to their friends. On the previous page is an example of a flier with a fax order form on the back. Notice how much it looks like the ad.

Use Postcards and Mailing Houses

A relative of the newsletter is the postcard. It is an even quicker read. Because studies show readers digest information in a 'Z' pattern, make sure you place your attention grabbing sentence across the top, your graphic or text in the middle and the most important information in the bottom right corner. Think of any movie ad. The headline quote grabs us; we then see what the quote refers to in a graphic. As we want to know more, we see where the movie is playing before turning the page. Your postcard, like an ad, must be structured the same way whether in black and white or color.

A word about mailing houses—use them. Business owners frequently don't because they *think* mailing it themselves is cheaper, but it frequently costs them more. Why? Because a good mailing house will review your material and suggest ways to save money; they'll barcode and pre-sort your list so your postcards can be mailed for the lowest available rate. The difference per piece more than makes up for the cost of the mailing service.

Find the Right Vehicle to Drive Your Message

Never let someone else determine your marketing. One of my favorite examples of this common mistake is from Bryan Johnson at Haute Links. For many months he had been running a *Penny Saver* ad offering a discount, but he had seen no growth in sales. When I asked him why he continued to run it, he gave me a simple reason. An ad representative had called on him and offered to design his ad for free. For a minimal monthly sum, he thought he was reaching his target market.

I seriously doubted if the BMW driving diners we saw in his parking lot read the *Penny Saver*, much less responded to discount ads. Especially since Bryan is located in a high-tech area of a very prosperous neighborhood. He dropped that advertising vehicle at once, and I created a new campaign in an upscale publication that focused on the white-collar workers who surrounded his store.

Lots of sales representatives call on you trying to sell you on a *great* vehicle for your particular business. But whether it is the people who do door hangars, the people who put coupons on the back of register receipts or the people who sell ads on bus benches, it all comes back to the same thing. You know who your customers are. If you've done your homework, you'll know right away if a vehicle is right for you.

Focus Print Ads within Your Market

Anyone within two miles of your establishment needs to know where you are. You need to spend money to lock up this immediate market. Therefore, concentrate your ads in neighborhood papers that are only circulated within a two-mile radius of your store. Their prices will be less, so you can run more often and target the people most likely to shop with you. Avoid taking out an expensive ad that reaches too broad a market until your customer demographics justify it.

Sponsor Community Events

Sponsorship by itself does not bring in new customers, but sponsorship does make people who already shop with you feel good about what you are contributing to their community.

Sponsorship has many forms. The best gives you face-to-face time with your target audience. Look for opportunities to put your face and your product in front of potential customers. From kids to AIDS to breast cancer, all are worthy causes. How do you decide?

As a good neighbor, you do have to participate in the events and causes in your community. First, though, find out exactly what the organization does; you don't want to be surprised when your name is linked with someone you abhor.

This is strategic marketing; you need to think about who will be attending the upcoming event. A black-tie, silent auction at the mayor's residence would attract a different crowd than a local church's pancake breakfast. Because you know who your customers are, you'll know which event more of your customers will likely attend. The people who need to see you out in the community are the people who already have a relationship with your business.

Keep a record of any and all donations, whether product, time or resources, in one place so you can review the total donations at the end of the year—you might be surprised at the total dollars you gave away. The following year you can budget these worthwhile causes.

Finally, if you sponsor an event, make sure your logo shows up in all its advertising. Ask for a proof to make sure there are no mistakes in logo colors or the spelling of your name.

Craft Press Releases that Work

Many businesses complain that the local papers don't print their news releases. There's a simple reason: no story. One paragraph about a sale or your anniversary is much less likely to be published than one that highlights an award you or an employee has received.

A press release announcing a new drink is less likely to gain attention if you can't tell a story about how you came up with it and how it has grown in popularity.

Sponsorship of community events is a start, but you need to think like a reporter. Where is the angle for a story? If your business is catering a dinner and one of your employees is featured as part of the entertainment, write the press release with some interesting quotes from the employee and send it to the paper at least a month in advance of the event. While it may never be picked up, you've made it easy for the reporter who is on deadline to either print it verbatim or contact you for additional information. Either way, you win.

The first paragraph of a press release should always include the who, what, when, why and how of an event. The next paragraph should include some type of quote that illuminates more of the story. The final paragraph should include a background of your business and ways to contact you. It should all be double-spaced and take up no more than two pages. The following is a press release I used to announce the coffeehouse alliance.

AUGUST 14, 2000   CONTACT: BOB PHIBBS
FOR IMMEDIATE RELEASE   562-555-2996

Independent Coffeehouses Form
Alliance to Combat Chains

LONG BEACH—Three of the city's most recognized independently owned and operated coffeehouses have come together and formed the *Long Beach Independent Coffee House Alliance*. Marty Cox, owner of **It's A Grind Coffee House**, Gary Paterno, co-owner of **The Library Coffeehouse** and Mike Sheldrake, owner of **Polly's Gourmet Coffee** announced today that the alliance was formed to raise consumer awareness by sharing advertising and pooling resources to gain greater exposure in the Long Beach market. While all three have varied atmospheres from the **Library Coffeehouse's** classic Bohemian look and cozy setting, to the open patio and Mission style furniture of **Polly's Gourmet Coffee** to the upscale slate covered walls and comfortable conversation areas of **It's A Grind**, these owners are uniting to speak out on the proliferation of chain stores. "We're doing the same thing a community does when they see something happening in their neighborhood that needs attention," began Paterno. "The three of us are working together to raise the level of specialty coffee and remind our customers that they have a choice of atmospheres as different as the neighborhoods

–More–

we are located in," continued Sheldrake. "And we're the ones who opened stores in the communities we believed in, the communities where I grew up. These same communities apparently did not meet **Starbucks** criteria, until now," Cox continued. "It is up to us to make sure our local customers know that we are building community between these three independent businesses, just like our coffee houses have helped build community gathering places for years."

Polly's Gourmet Coffee began in 1976 as the only specialty coffee roaster between Beverly Hills and San Diego. Polly's fight with **Starbucks** has been featured on PBS and in both the *Los Angeles Times* and *New York Times*. **It's A Grind Coffee House**, established in 1995, operates five coffeehouses in Long Beach. A **Starbucks** is either under construction or in lease negotiations to open across from four of the five **It's A Grind stores**; near one location, they're rumored to be opening two. **The Library Coffeehouse**, featured in Los Angeles magazine as "Best in LA" was started in 1993.

For information regarding the *Long Beach Independent Coffee House Alliance*, contact spokesman Bob Phibbs, 562-555-2996.

#

Once you send out the press release, follow up with a call to the reporter within a few days. Always ask first if they are on deadline and if they say *yes*, ask when you can call back—never push a reporter. It is always a good idea to include a photo with your press release. Stick a label on the back that identifies the people pictured. Make sure to include your contact phone number.

If you really want a story done, get creative. Once I hand delivered a custom cake to the head of the features department of the *Los Angeles Times* with a personal message on it and a press kit. While the recipient said, "Gifts are strictly forbidden," I found out later he enjoyed the treat and my story ran. Press relations, like customers, are all based on relationships.

Get a Website

You must have a website. At a bare minimum, it must have your name and logo, address, your concise business description, hours of operation and phone with email address. While it doesn't have to be fancy or multi-media, this is *your* image to the world. Include examples of your products and testimonials from customers.

As a specialty retailer, the product lines you carry will bring people to you who have never heard of you before. A website is a good way to service customers who move away or who visit you from out of town. A good website also provides customers with a way to offer feedback about their experience in your store.

Your .com name is extremely important. You want an easy name to make it easy for customers to find you. Their first inclination will be to enter www.yourname.com. But with the new .com names added every day across the world, there is a good chance it may be gone. You'll need to think creatively to get around this obstacle. For example if Pollys.com is taken, then pollyscoffee.com might be a good alternative.

That said, when I established the Bay Shores Inn website three years ago, I had to take a different tact. An inn in Vermont had already taken Bayshoresinn.com along with several other names people might try. The hyphen, dash, slash derivatives added confusion. I came up with a whole new approach: thebestinn.com. After we had that established, I looked for other .com names we could register to use as pointers to our site. These names have expanded to include seven longer names like bestwesternnewportbeach.com. While I don't expect people to enter them directly, those .com names are all registered with the different search engines and directories. This increases the likelihood that a customer browsing the net will be referred to our site since search engines look for .com names first and then the description.

Websites reach new customers through the web search engines and directories: Yahoo, Alta Vista, etc. To register your site with these companies, you will need about twenty key search-words that describe your business and your location. For Polly's Gourmet Coffee I included coffee, coffee beans, roast coffee, gourmet coffee, espresso, coffeehouse, gifts and Long Beach. Search the Internet using the words you've come up with and see what the search engines find. If you are resourceful, you can log onto a competitor's site and see their key search-words. Borrow what works for you.

Having said all this, I hire professional web designers to create, service register and run my websites. I don't have the time, background or inclination to try and reinvent the wheel. Generally, neither do you.

If You Use Signs, Make Them Special

Frequently, banners are used by businesses to tout a discount or sale. Resist the urge. If you must put one up, think of your banners and signs as another form of advertising, and use the same guidelines as to content and white space. Feature only one idea.

When Starbucks hung their *Now Open* sign across the street from It's A Grind, Marty Cox wanted to put up a counter banner. I came up with one that I really liked, but I needed a bit of information.

First, I called Starbucks headquarters in Seattle and said I was doing a story about their new store opening, did they know what number it was? (All year we'd seen articles about Starbucks having 2200 stores in the US, and I figured that had to be low.) The answer came back that it was the 5,565th. I asked, so you mean there are 5,564 others? Yes. With that information, I created my banner to read:

It's A Grind
With the 5565th Starbucks
Across the Street

We included our logo and all their copyright information at the bottom to protect ourselves legally. We put the sign up on the parkway in front of the store. People talked about it for weeks.

A bit of creativity made the sign much more powerful than a generally worded *stop in for an iced mocha* with a price would ever have done.

One final thought, if you are going to use banners, know when to take them down. When I did a store evaluation in March one year, a green and red banner was still drooped across the front of their store. It said *Holiday Gift Specials*.

Put Up a Billboard Across From The Chain

You can't afford to blanket your hometown with ads, fliers and mailers like the big chains can, but you might be able to buy one strategically placed billboard. Knowing how many cars drove down a main street, my brother Gerry who ran a hardware in Glendale, CA put up a large billboard right outside of Home Depot. As Home Depot customers walked out, they saw his billboard with pictures of his smiling employees. Below the headline *Couldn't find what you were looking for?* was a bright red arrow pointing up the street to his store. That one sign netted him a lot of new customers. If you can find the perfect place, put up the perfect sign.

Wait On TV and Trade Radio

TV is great for national chains but probably not for you. I learned this when I produced a cable spot for Polly's Gourmet Coffee which ran for three weeks on the local cable channels including CNN, HGTV, the Food Network and A&E. Although it was a good commercial, we simply didn't have the resources to have the ad run more than once an hour on an occasional basis. Unless you have lots of money, wait on TV. If you do have lots of money, you need several impressions per hour to achieve any measurable results. Choose only a few programs but buy lots of airtime when your customers are likely to see it—not at two in the morning.

Radio can be pricey too, but you can often strike a deal and trade airtime for product. If you have a local jazz station whose demographics line up with yours, see if you can trade some of your product for an exclusive endorsement. If you are a nursery, sponsor a weekend garden show for your local radio station. If you are in auto repair, sponsor a live remote broadcast and car clinic. Be creative, and look for ways to find your niche customers in your area without squandering huge amounts of capital.

Tit for Tat—Here's When to Advertise

If a competitor places an ad in a local paper, you must answer it immediately with one of your own. If you are celebrating an anniversary, let your community know. Is someone making a special appearance? Talk it up. Did you do an extensive remodel? Invite us to see it. Remember, people forget you're around unless you get your name in front of them on a consistent basis. Christmas advertising is a given.

Go Where Your Strongest Customer Group Goes

Let's review—the best use of your marketing money is to hold on to current customers with thank you notes, postcards and newsletters. Those in turn will lead your existing customers to tell their friends about you. Then, to attract new customers to your store, match up your demographics with what vehicles you can use to get your message out there.

If you have a customer base that is predominantly moms and kids, an ad in the local school newspaper might be a good use of your money, but an ad in the local business journal would not. If you have a customer base that includes a significant senior citizen contingent, an ad in their local community center's newsletter would be a good use of your money. If you have a customer base that typically goes to the symphony, goes to the tractor pull or mounts an annual holiday show, look for ways to find them and their friends. When you are in your store, ask customers where they went last weekend or where they are going this weekend. Then go to these events and look around for new customers. Find out where they spend their time and money and, like the big boxes, get in front of them.

How NOT to Advertise

Eight months into my contract with Polly's Gourmet Coffee, a group of CSULB students analyzed my marketing efforts. 75 percent of the thousand people they polled knew our marketing campaign. This wasn't a huge surprise to me. Remember, *Down the Street From Ordinary* was on all of our logoed cups, on every ad, on bumper stickers, on fliers and in our newsletter.

As the students presented their findings, they also included a few recommendations. One was to offer coupons. "Are they still teaching that crap?" I asked.

The stunned student sheepishly said, "Yes," and then shot back at me, "Well, how else do you know if your ads work?"

I laughed and said, "Sales are up 40 percent—I think they're working. And sorry, no coupon is going to show me if they are bringing in new business, just who used a coupon."

I never recommend a coupon or a discount for anyone who does not already have a positive relationship with their business.

My very first business evaluation was for a pizza store in Costa Mesa, CA. After asking a lot of questions, I was told by the manager, "You don't understand, this is a coupon driven business. We have to discount or we won't be in business." There was nothing special about the service or the atmosphere, although the pizza was excellent. I said in my report, "If the only way you can get people in the door is by continually discounting your product, you have no profit to balance the promotion. You do not have a going concern. You must change immediately and stress your quality of pizza, location and other strengths." When I presented the evaluation, the owner shared with me that the business had never been profitable.

Don't Discount a Premium Product

One of the things I did at both Polly's Gourmet Coffee and the Bay Shores Inn was to discontinue any discount programs. In fact, I *raised* their prices. One owner was skeptical of such an idea; after all, any money in the register was *money in his jeans*. I told him that if we say we are a boutique inn or a gourmet coffeehouse, there is a perception of something special, a premium location or gourmet product offered. Once it is discounted, the cachet of the product is cheapened. The competitive edge is gone.

Untrained marketers who say *we need to do something* always go the easy *let's discount* way. It takes very little imagination and since everybody else does it, they assume it must work.

I held a contest at It's A Grind for employees to come up with ways they thought we could get new business. 90 percent of their ideas had something to do with giving a discount, either a two-for-one coupon or a giveaway of a premium drink.

I will admit that certain coupons can bring in business much like spot sales can boost your numbers. The problem is that you are in dangerous waters; the icebergs are numerous.

Here are seven reasons coupons don't work:
- Coupons are looked at as an ongoing effort. In effect, they become the whole marketing plan.
- By the time you factor in your time in creating them, printing them, distributing them and factoring in the actual discounting itself, you have a very expensive promotion.
- You have taught the customer that your product is not worth what you priced it at.
- The people who found you through coupons will wait for your next one.
- You are rewarding people who have no relationship to the success of your business.
- Your sales staff will keep a copy of the coupon to offer to their own customers or friends.
- If your regular customers who have supported you find out someone who's never been there is getting a better deal than they are, they just might not return.

That's precisely what happened at a local restaurant in Long Beach where a group of us went for a birthday celebration. Located in an old craftsman house with antiques and a wood-burning fireplace, this was a great place to enjoy a great meal. We had ordered wine before dinner, enjoyed fabulous entrees and saved room for their signature desserts.

When the couple at the table next to us paid their check with a 50 percent off coupon, the owner must have been tipped off. He went to their table and sat down. We overheard him talk about his participation in the 50 percent off Entertainment Book. He said that he valued the Entertainment Book because it brought in customers who had never tried him before. He told them the story of his business and how many years he'd been there. They told him they were from Pacoima, about an hour's drive from the restaurant and that they would never have come without the coupon. He smiled, wished them well and said he looked forward to seeing them again.

I was incensed! We lived in the neighborhood. We'd gone there for years, paid top dollar and received no special recognition. *How did we feel? Who was more important?* Here we had paid full price as usual and the people next to us who had no relationship paid half-price. I haven't been back since.

I've used this story many times in my presentations. At a dinner part,. I told it to someone who admitted using the Entertainment Book. She told me she only patronizes that restaurant with a coupon. The owner has taught her that his menu is not worth full price. So where does the profit come from? *He'll raise prices for his loyal customers to offset his coupons to his one-time discount hunters!*

Anyone can be a discount whore; it takes no brains or skill. There is no forethought. No magic or relationship results. And once you do it, you're often condemned to repeating it.

Cut your prices repeatedly and you'd better cut your staff because profit is what suffers.

A struggling coffee house in Long Beach ran a variation of this ad every week. Look at all the things wrong with it from logo, offer, clutter and intent. This is how to waste your ad budget with coupons. And by the way, they recently closed.

Price Ads—The Easy Way Out

Clearly the easiest ad to create is the price ad, a photo or graphic of the product with a cheap price by it. Price ads are used frequently with no salesmanship involved at the store level. You don't have to train your sales crew about a $2.99 widget pictured in a price ad. A customer sees it and theoretically buys it, no questions asked. Most businesses use price ads exclusively because their eyes have never been opened to other possibilities.

Inexperienced marketers add coupons to these ads to try and justify the success of the campaign. *These coupons only prove that there are bargain hunters out there.* Just because they come to your store this time doesn't mean they will again unless they have a coupon. *These are not the loyal regular customers that you can build a business on.*

Don't Annoy People with Telemarketing

I continue to be amazed that the telemarketing industry survives! They break into people's homes uninvited, usually at the dinner hour or on a relaxing weekend. Never hire a company to do it for you. Even worse are the machines that do it automatically! I strenuously advise everyone not to participate in this all out assault on privacy. This of course, does not include you personally calling customers who have willingly given you their number to keep in touch about new arrivals and such.

* * *

You will never know *conclusively* if a campaign is working, no matter what anyone tells you. Customers come in for lots of reasons including great customer service, a need for your specific product

> There really isn't any mystery in how to market a business. You just need to know who you are, who you want to be, who your customers are and how to talk to them. Then you need to do it!

and your clever ads. To try and separate one from the other to justify an ad budget is missing the point.

Customers seldom come in only because they saw just one ad. Good ad campaigns are a series of impressions and are built in layers. To successfully survive, an independent retailer must use all of the marketing layers she or he can.

But you don't want to call attention to a business that hasn't taken care of the basics. Otherwise, you'll get people to come in and try you, only to be disappointed. Know how many friends they'll tell about their disappointment? Ten.

CHAPTER 10

You *Can* Compete

Many retailers don't see the competition as anything requiring them to change. On the contrary, they often continue business as usual. Again, this is the *hubris* spoken about in Greek tragedies, the feeling that you can do whatever you want or that you are invincible from the inevitable outcome of your actions.

While a customer may not complain, *hubris* adds frustration to the shopping experience. Retailers epitomize it, believing they can operate without consequence. They foolishly believe business will always be theirs. The customer and their purchases are taken for granted.

Customers may go to the new big-box stores but they usually come back to the independent, even though the independent may not be as shiny and new.

Customers in your store aren't willing to search and search for what they want. You must either have knowledgeable salespeople or your signage must clearly point the way. You cannot have items in your store that aren't labeled or priced. Customers stay if the little stuff is taken care of. They leave if they're frustrated.

People who own their own businesses are more likely to fall into bad behaviors because there is no one holding them accountable. And when business starts trailing off, many independents call on other independent retailers for their spin. Having your eyes squarely focused on how everyone else is doing is a recipe for disaster. To succeed, you must focus solely on your own business and how you can improve the experience for your customers and employees.

It really doesn't matter if another store is doing better or worse than you are. If you call up another retailer and ask how business is and she says *great* and yours isn't, it will only make you feel worse. If she says *lousy* and yours is too, you'll only commiserate and uselessly analyze the situation. Finally, if you call her and she says, *lousy* and yours is *great* she won't want to talk to you. None of these exchanges will help make your business better!

It is easy for the independent to place all the blame on the big-box retailer. When sales fall off, some independents say, "They're all on the Internet or at (fill in the name of a big-box retailer)." It is easy to lose faith in your customers when you know they've seen something better and you've been taking them for granted.

People will give you a second and even a third chance if they know you care about them. Not taking care of your facility means you don't care about your customer. Burned out bulbs, dusty shelves and shabby employees all add up to a disregard for the customer's experience.

The moment of truth arrives for the independent retailer when a customer makes a special request or has a problem and the retailer doesn't take it seriously. *Sorry* just doesn't work anymore. You need to have systems and processes in place to minimize things falling through the cracks.

The big-box retailers are trying to provide a better experience for everyone. That's why they spend such big bucks on store layout, design, product display and getting their logo everywhere. They know the stakes are high.

Now that you too realize how high the stakes are, you must put your merchandise out where it can best be featured rather than wherever there is space. You must work to hire and train only the best employees. You must market smarter.

You must be focused, you must be consistent and you must be creative. After having addressed your facility, sales and then your marketing, you will have developed a consistent image from start to finish which will give you the advantage over the big chains.

There is no Bruce Willis who is going to come in and save you. There is no magic that just having read this book, you'll automatically change. You need to realize that at this point, you can be as happy and successful as you make your mind up to be.

However, if you are more secure bitching about how unfair business is, you probably will have finished this and said, "Big deal, I knew most of that." For you the ship sank long ago. Now it is just a matter of time before you realize you have been asleep at the helm and that your customers are not coming back.

However, if your back is against the wall like Mike Sheldrake's was in 1998, you'll take what I've taught you as your custom blueprint toward making your business successful.

The independent business owner's worst fear is going out of business, that it will be taken away or that she can't hold on long enough to change.

Hopefully in this book, you have learned it is the attitude you bring to the challenge that will ultimately make you successful. You are living the American dream. Thousands of people wish they too could have the guts to own their own business.

Use what I have taught you right now. Do something and get started! Don't get overwhelmed. Just see if you can identify what needs to be improved. If so, you're halfway there. If you can't see it, call me; the *Retail Doctor* makes house calls.

Whatever you do, don't do a story in the local paper about how you can't compete *because you can*. You're not sunk; you now have a life ring. Good selling!

Acknowledgments

To Nancy Himel, the muse who provided the necessary direction, order, patience and editing skills to make this book flow;

Bill Pratt for his sharp insights into what was important and what wasn't as my first reader;

Mike Sheldrake who took a chance on a stranger helping him, a process that benefited both of us;

All of my clients who have embraced these ideas and proven they work;

All the employees who it has been my privilege to learn from over the past thirty years.

Thank you all.

About the Author

Bob Phibbs, the *Retail Doctor*, has helped hundreds of small and medium sized businesses in the hospitality, restaurant and retail industries. He and his work have been featured on Public Broadcasting's *Life and Times*, in *Entrepreneur* magazine, the *Wall Street Journal* and the *New York Times*. In addition, Phibbs provides business makeovers for the *Los Angeles Times*. From his headquarters in Long Beach, CA, he has creatively helped businesses succeed when their customer base has been challenged.

A sought-after public speaker and trainer, Phibbs regularly addresses business organizations, corporations and business conferences. His presentations are designed to challenge business owners to *look in the mirror* to see how to compete.

One of Phibbs' most publicized successes was in Long Beach where sales had slipped for years after Starbucks opened ten blocks away from an independent coffeehouse owner. When a second Starbucks opened just seventy-five feet from his store in 1998, the *Retail Doctor* was brought in to overhaul the operation. Sales rose a dramatic 50 percent over that record year and an additional 40 percent the following year.

As an active leader in the Long Beach community, Mr. Phibbs is frequently quoted on matters relating to how independent retailers can succeed and is a member of the National Speaker's Association.

Notes

Notes

Notes